VanThanh Productions in association with Park Theatre
presents the World Premiere of

Summer
Rolls

By Tuyen Do
Directed by **Kristine Landon-Smith**
Set & Costume Design by **Moi Tran**

T0348010

SUMMER ROLLS
By Tuyen Do

CAST (in order of appearance)
Mother/Woman **Linh-Dan Pham**
Son **Christopher Nguyen**
Anh **Michael Phong Le**
Mai **Anna Nguyen**
Mr Dinh **David Lee-Jones**
Father/Man **Kwong Loke**
David **Keon Martial-Phillip**

CREATIVE TEAM
Director **Kristine Landon-Smith**
Dramaturg **Sudha Bhuchar**
Producer **Tuyet Van Huynh**
Lighting Designer **Jessica Hung Han Yun**
Sound Designer **Nicola Chang**
Set & Costume Designer **Moi Tran**
Assistant Director **Charlotte Everest**
Assistant Producer **Zhui Ning Chang**
Exhibition Photographer **Caro Gervay**
Production Manager **Dan Gosselin**
Scenic Constructor **KD Productions**
Stage Manager **Natalie Wong**
Production Assistant **Deanna Dzulkifli**
Lx Programmer **Raycher Phua**
Movement Facilitator **Christina Kapadocha**
Costume Assistant **Yiran Duan**
Design Assistant **Mona Camille**
Design Assistant **Erin Guan**
Graphic Designer **Emilie Chen**
Marketing Manager **Tara Parashar**
Production Photographer **Dante Kim**
Videographer **Paul Burt**

CAST

DAVID LEE-JONES Dinh

Theatre roles include: *Skin in Flames* (Park Theatre), *#aiww: The Arrest of Ai Weiwei* (Hampstead Theatre), *The Grammar of Love* (Ovalhouse), the 50th anniversary production of Noël Coward's *Waiting in the Wings* (WYNI), *Chicken* (Hackney Empire), *The Illegals* (Ice and Fire), *A Midsummer Night's Dream* (Southwark Playhouse), *Burning Maps* (Outside Edge), and *Back to Methuselah* (MFP). He has completed four national/international tours with acclaimed outdoor Shakespeare specialists The Festival Players – as Richard in *Richard III*, Antonio in *The Merchant of Venice*, Benedick in *Much Ado About Nothing*, and Rosalind in an all-male *As You Like It*.

Screen credits include: *The Complex* (Little Jade Productions/ Red & Black Films), *Apeiron* (Double Negative), *The Backseat* (Hidden Art Films), and upcoming comedy feature *Elevator Gods* (Happy Our Films).

KWONG LOKE Father

Theatre credits include: *Pah-La* (Royal Court); *The Great Wave* (National Theatre); *Labour of Love* (Noel Coward, West End); *Dear Elizabeth* (Gate Theatre); *New and Now* (Royal Court); *You For Me For You* (Royal Court); *You Never Touched Dirt* (Royal Court at Edinburgh); *The Lulu Plays* (Almeida Theatre); *Hiawatha* (Bristol Old Vic); *Global Baby Factory* (Yellow Earth Theatre); *The Changeling* (Finborough Theatre); *Rashomon, Scenes from Paradise* (Riverside Studios); *The Magic Paintbrush, The Snow Lion* (Polka Theatre); *Blue Remembered Hills* (UK Tour); *Tibetan Inroads* (Gate Theatre); *Two Gentlemen of Verona* (Singapore Drama Centre), and *The Soldier's Tale* (Southbank Centre).

TV credits include: *The Feed* (ITV Amazon); *Gangs of London* (HBO-Sky); *As Time Goes By, Love Hurts, Blue Peter, Casualty, The Knock, Loose* and *The Monkey King*.

KEON MARTIAL-PHILLIP David

Keon trained at the Oxford School of Drama. Theatre credits include: *Pool (no water)* (Royal Court); and *Children of Killers* (Orange Tree Theatre). *Summer Rolls* is Keon's professional debut.

ANNA NGUYEN Mai

Anna trained at the Royal Central School of Speech and Drama (BA Collaborative and Devised Theatre) and at the Brit School. Radio credits include: *They Call Us Viet Kieu* and *When Heaven and Earth Changed Places* (Greenpoint Productions). *Summer Rolls* is Anna's theatrical debut.

CHRISTOPHER NGUYEN Young Anh

Screen credits include: *Star Wars: Episode VII – The Force Awakens* (LucasFilms); *Next Time* (Film London); *Healthy* (Hades Productions) and various commercials. *Summer Rolls* is Christopher's theatrical debut.

LINH-DAN PHAM Mother

Theatre credits include: international productions such as *The Buddha In The Attic* (Festival d'Avignon); *Les Justes* (Théâtre du Chêne Noir); *Crossing Rockaway Parkway* (The Sanford Meisner Theatre) and *Wills & Secession* (Fort Canning Theatre).

Film credits include: *The Beat My Heart Skipped* (won BAFTA); *The Terrible Privacy of Maxwell Sim*, *Les Yeux Fermés*, *Adrift/Choi Voi*, *Tout Ce Qui Brille*, *Le Bal Des Actrices*, *Ninja Assassin*, *Mr Nobody* and *Indochine* (won Oscar, Golden Globe and César).

TV credits include: *Casualty, One Child, Pigalle La Nuit, Trial & Retribution, This Life – Ten Years Later,* and *Farewell To Song Ba.*

MICHAEL PHONG LE Anh

Theatre credits include: *Forgotten* (Arcola Theatre & Theatre Royal Plymouth) and *The Autumn of Han* (Red Dragonfly Productions). Michael wrote and performed his own play *Khon* which won the Taking Flight Festival and will be transferring to the Edinburgh Fringe Festival.

TV credits include: *The Catherine Tate Show* (BBC); *DCI Banks* (ITV) and *Hooten & The Lady* (Sky).

He trained at Royal Birmingham Conservatoire.

CREATIVE TEAM

SUDHA BHUCHAR Dramaturg

Sudha is an award-winning actor/playwright/founder of Bhuchar Boulevard. As co-founder of Tamasha, with Kristine Landon-Smith, they made landmark work including *A Fine Balance* and the award-winning musical *Fourteen Songs, Two Weddings and a Funeral*. Other acclaimed plays include *Child of the Divide* (Asian Media Awards 2018) and *My Name is...*, which Sudha also adapted for Radio 4. Sudha's acting credits include Gurpreet Bhatti's *Khandan* (Royal Court and Birmingham Rep) and *The Village* by April de Angelis (Theatre Royal Stratford East).

TV includes *Coronation Street* and the upcoming *Noughts and Crosses*. Film includes Disney's *Mary Poppins Returns* and Ben Wheatley's *Happy New Year Colin Burstead*. Sudha won a Tongues on Fire Flame Award (2018) and was a finalist for BBC Radio 4's Audio Drama Awards (2019) for *My Son the Doctor* (co-written with Saleyha Ahsan). As dramaturg, Sudha recently worked with Nyla Levy on *Does My Bomb Look Big In This?*

NICOLA CHANG Sound Designer

Nicola Chang is a composer/sound designer for theatre, film and commercial media across the UK, US and Asia. She has been playing percussion and piano for 20 years, and plays for *Six* (West End) and *STOMP!* (West End/World Tour). She is also an Artistic Associate of the King's Head Theatre and a BFI x BAFTA Crew Member. She was nominated for two Off-West End Awards in Sound Design last award season. In 2017, she conducted the London Film Music Orchestra playing her original soundtracks (accompanied with live screenings), and premiered her concerto for Ping Pong and Piano Trio at the Queen Elizabeth Hall in January 2019; this concerto will be performed in Shanghai later this year. She is also attached to the British Youth Music Theatre UK as a Composer and Musical Director.

TUYEN DO Writer

Tuyen Do is a British East Asian writer, actor, and workshop facilitator. She has been part of the Royal Court's studio writing group, Tamasha Playwrights, and Bristol Old Vic's 2016/17 open session writers' programme.

Her work has been performed with Tamasha Theatre, Kali Theatre, and Yellow Earth Theatre. Tuyen has also written for short film projects, including *Healthy* which won an honourable mention for Best Short at the Asians On Film Festival 2014. Much of her creative work stems from her British Vietnamese roots. *Summer Rolls* is Tuyen's full-length playwriting debut.

JESSICA HUNG HAN YUN Lighting Designer

Jessica Hung is a London-based lighting designer specialising in interior and exterior installations, fashion, circus, events, theatre, festivals and dance.

Her credits include *Equus* (English Touring Theatre and Theatre Royal Stratford East, Offie nomination for Lighting Design); *Pah-La* (Royal Court); *Armadillo* (Yard Theatre); *Nine Foot Nine* (Bunka, Offie nomination for Lighting Design); *Nonsuch Theatre Company* (Lakeside Theatre Nottingham); *Dear Elizabeth* & *The Human Voice* (Gate Theatre); *Hive City Legacy* (Roundhouse); *Forgotten* (Arcola Theatre) and *Cuckoo* (Soho Theatre).

TUYET VAN HUYNH Producer

Tuyet Van Huynh is a theatre producer, film programmer and curator whose focus is to create safe spaces for Vietnamese creatives and communities. She is also one of the co-founders of BEATS, an organisation founded by British East Asians in Theatre and on Screen championing equality and representation for BEAs in the industry. Tuyet previously worked as a Digital Producer at the National Theatre's Immersive Storytelling Studio. In 2015 she ran a two-year project, *Kinima*, programming iconic cult films and curating live performances as part of a 'cine-variety' film experience that ran at London's Cinema Museum. Tuyet will curate the first British Vietnamese Film Festival launching in summer next year.

KRISTINE LANDON-SMITH Director

Kristine Landon-Smith began her career as an actor and moved into directing and teaching in the early years of her professional life. She co-founded Tamasha Theatre in 1989 and as Co-Artistic Director directed all but one of the company's shows.

Her 1996 production of *East is East* was nominated for an Olivier award and her original production of *Fourteen Songs, Two Weddings and A Funeral* won the Barclays Theatre Award for Best New Musical. Whilst at Tamasha she also held a position as producer of Radio Drama for BBC Radio 4 and produced and directed plays, short stories and serials for Radio 3, 4 and the World Service. In 2013 Kristine stepped out of Tamasha to take up a Senior Lecturer position at the National Institute of Dramatic Art in Australia which she held for three years. She has been freelancing in industry and the Conservatoire training space since her return in 2016, and has worked for a range of organisations including East 15, LAMDA, Mountview, SOAS, Drama Centre, Cardboard Citizens and Dukes Playhouse Lancaster.

MOI TRAN Set & Costume Designer

Moi Tran is a creative designer whose work spans theatre, dance, opera, film, animation, site-specific installation and other disciplines. Moi trained at the Motley School of Design, Winchester School of Art, and is currently completing her Masters in Fine Arts at The Chelsea College of Art. She is one of the 2017/18 Old Vic 12 cohort.

Her theatre credits include *White Pearl* (Royal Court); *Dear Elizabeth* (Gate Theatre); *Under the Umbrella* (Yellow Earth Theatre); *Deluge* (Hampstead Theatre) and *The Manual Oracle* (Yard Theatre). She also works as a designer for the Guardian and Observer newspapers.

VanThanh Productions
Tuyen Do & Tuyet Huynh Producers

VanThanh Productions was established by Tuyen Do and Tuyet Huynh in 2018. Their mission is to enable minority groups to tell their own stories. Their first production is *Summer Rolls* at Park Theatre 2019.

About Park Theatre

Park Theatre was founded by Artistic Director, Jez Bond and Associate Artistic Director, Melli Marie. The building opened in May 2013 and, with four West End transfers, two National Theatre transfers and ten national tours in its first five years, quickly garnered a reputation as a key player in the London theatrical scene. Park Theatre has received four Olivier nominations, won Offie Awards for Best New Play, Best Set Design and Best Foodie Experience, and won The Stage's Fringe Theatre of the Year in 2015.

Park Theatre is an inviting and accessible venue, delivering work of exceptional calibre in the heart of Finsbury Park. We work with writers, directors and designers of the highest quality to present compelling, exciting and beautifully told stories across our two intimate spaces.

Our programme encompasses a broad range of work from classics to revivals with a healthy dose of new writing, producing in-house as well as working in partnership with emerging and established producers. We strive to play our part within the UK's theatre ecology by offering mentoring, support and opportunities to artists and producers within a professional theatre-making environment.

Our Creative Learning strategy seeks to widen the number and range of people who participate in theatre, and provides opportunities for those with little or no prior contact with the arts.

In everything we do we aim to be warm and inclusive; a safe, welcoming and wonderful space in which to work, create and visit.

★★★★★ 'A five-star neighbourhood theatre.' *The Independent*

As a registered charity [number 1137223] with no public subsidy, we rely on the kind support of our donors and volunteers. To find out how you can get involved visit parktheatre.co.uk

For Park Theatre

Artistic Director | Jez Bond
Executive Director | Rachael Williams
Associate Artistic Director | Melli Marie
Development Director | Dorcas Morgan
Sales & Marketing Director | Dawn James
Sales & Marketing Manager | Rachel McCall
Finance Manager | Elaine Lavelle
Finance & Administration Officer | Susie Italiano
Development & Production Assistant | Daniel Cooper
Technical and Buildings Manager | Sacha Queiroz
Deputy Technical and Buildings Manager | Neal Gray
Administrator | Melissa Bonnelame
Community Engagement Manager | Nina Graveney-Edwards
Access Coordinator | Sarah Howard
Venue & Volunteer Manager | Barry Card
Deputy Venue & Volunteer l Michael Peavoy
Duty Venue Managers | Abigail Acons-Grocock, Natasha Green, Shaun Joynson
Head of Food and Beverage | Brett Reynolds
Food and Beverage Senior Supervisor | Oli Mortimer
Cafe Bar Team | Grace Boateng, Robert Czibi, Gemma Barnet, Josh Oakes Rodgers, Amy Conway, Matt Littleson, Ryan Peek, Alice Pegram, Ewan Brand, Adam Harding Kheir, Sebastian Harker, Jack Mosedale, Maisie Saidgrove, Florence Blackmore, Kerry Hunt, James Bradwell, Yan Tobi-Amisi
Senior Box Office Supervisor | Natasha Green
Box Office Supervisors | Greg Barnes, Natalie Chan, Holly McComish, Jack Mosedale, Libby Nash, Nathalie Saunders and Alex Whitlock

Public Relations | Nick Pearce and Julie Holman for Target Live

President | Jeremy Bond

Ambassadors
David Horovitch
Celia Imrie
Sean Mathias
Tanya Moodie
Hattie Morahan
Tamzin Outhwaite
Meera Syal

Associate Artist
Mark Cameron

Trustees
Andrew Cleland-Bogle
Nick Frankfort
Robert Hingley
Mars Lord
Sir Frank McLoughlin
Bharat Mehta
Rufus Olins
Nigel Pantling (Chair)
Victoria Phillips
Jo Parker

With thanks to all of our supporters, donors and volunteers.

A heartfelt thank you to

Kristine Landon-Smith and Sudha Bhuchar who have been with this play from its very seed. Thank you for your belief in the story and your unyielding passion to bringing unheard voices to the fore. So many artists past, present and future are forever indebted to you for shining a light on the path that did not exist before you.

Each brilliant actor, director, and dramaturg who helped me listen to the play during workshops and readings at Tamasha scratch night Rich Mix, Yellow Earth Typhoon reading Soho Theatre, and R&D readings at Tristan Bates and the Arnolfini in Bristol.

James Peries, Bristol Old Vic, who has been instrumental in helping the play receive its first full production. Thank you for your advice and support throughout.

Melli Marie at the Park Theatre for recognising and believing in the message of the play.

Arts Council England Project Grants support.

Tuyet Van Huynh, the other half of VanThanh Productions. Your generosity, tenacity and determination are contagious. I cannot imagine doing this journey without you.

To the entire cast and crew of *Summer Rolls* at the Park Theatre production.

Members of the Vietnamese community who have lent their time, advice and support. Cuong Pham, Dam Van Huynh, Lan Maika, Jack Shieh and Tai Huynh.

My beloved family who are my inspiration. Particularly my brothers and sisters whose support has been invaluable.

Roland, my husband. Our conversations have shaped my words and thinking. Thank you for your continued support and belief, without which none of this would be possible.

SUMMER ROLLS

Tuyền Đỗ

SUMMER ROLLS

OBERON BOOKS
LONDON

First published in 2019 by Oberon Books Ltd
521 Caledonian Road, London N7 9RH
Tel: +44 (0) 20 7607 3637 / Fax: +44 (0) 20 7607 3629
e-mail: info@oberonbooks.com
www.oberonbooks.com

Copyright © Tuyền Đỗ, 2019

Tuyền Đỗ is hereby identified as author of this play in accordance with section 77 of the Copyright, Designs and Patents Act 1988. The author has asserted her moral rights.

All rights whatsoever in this play are strictly reserved and application for performance etc. should be made before commencement of rehearsal to the author c/o Oberon Books (info@oberonbooks.com). No performance may be given unless a licence has been obtained, and no alterations may be made in the title or the text of the play without the author's prior written consent.

You may not copy, store, distribute, transmit, reproduce or otherwise make available this publication (or any part of it) in any form, or binding or by any means (print, electronic, digital, optical, mechanical, photocopying, recording or otherwise), without the prior written permission of the publisher.

A catalogue record for this book is available from the British Library.

PB ISBN: 9781786828040
E ISBN: 9781786828057

Cover concept by Émilie Chen / Cover photography by Gavin Li

eBook conversion by Lapiz Digital Services, India.

For
Ba Mẹ
and
Anh Hai

Characters

Notes

In the world of the play, all the Vietnamese characters (except Mai) are conversing with each other in fluent Vietnamese, but using English text.

Mai speaks actual Vietnamese poorly mixed with English to portray her struggle with the Vietnamese language.

When the children speak to each other, it is in English.

Text in **bold** is broken English with a strong Vietnamese accent.

David speaks in English. He does not speak Vietnamese.

Prologue

Vietnam, 1976. Near the Mekong river.

Under the cover of darkness, further camouflaged by overgrown banana leaves, a heavily pregnant WOMAN scuttles from tree to tree lit only by moonlight. Close behind her is a boy, 11 but small. Her SON. She tugs at his hand and pulls him near to her. A fishing vessel is waiting. He's sobbing.

WOMAN: Don't trust anybody. They will take everything you have.

SON: I don't want to / go.

WOMAN: When a chance comes along, you have to take it. Understand?

There is a noise. Flashlight. WOMAN gestures into the darkness that they are ready. She holds her SON, suddenly softer.

SON: I want to stay here / with you.

WOMAN: If you stay here, they will take you and make you fight for them. As soon as you're old enough, you'll be made to kill. I cannot lose you too.

SON: What will happen to you?

WOMAN: Don't worry about me.

SON: What will happen to her? *(Gestures at her tummy.)*

WOMAN: Her?

SON: I know it's a girl.

She pulls out a wad of dollars in plastic sewn into her áo bà ba (simple Vietnamese blouse) and starts to shove it down his pants.

WOMAN: I've sewn a pocket inside your pants. It can double up as an arse cushion. Everyone speaks the language of dollars.

SON: What if it the boat sinks?

WOMAN: It won't sink

SON: What if I fall?

WOMAN: You know how to swim.

SON: What if I don't make it.

She shakes him.

WOMAN: Fear is just a sign telling us we have to try harder.

SON nods.

You have to raise yourself up, my son. When you get to the other side. Say you're ten instead of eleven, no, nine, eight, the younger the better. They look after children... My prayers will keep you safe. I will wait for you. Even if it takes a thousand years. Now go.

She pushes him away. He refuses to leave.

SON: Mum.

WOMAN: You have a lucky number, my son.

There is another noise. Flashlight.

She shoves him hard away from her. He runs back and they embrace.

He runs into the darkness. WOMAN is left standing alone.

Her heart shatters and she lets out a stifled groan.

A swelling of sound.

The sea, mixed with sounds of human distress, the sound of a baby crying morphing into the indistinct sound of a crowd. Flashes of photographs of the future family and other Vietnamese faces litter the stage.

The Exhibition – Part One

The stage is lit with the photographs MAI has taken over the years. MAI in her mid-twenties visibly pregnant. It's the year 2002. She is in the spotlight. DAVID, smartly dressed, taps his glass and shouts.

DAVID: Everyone! Your attention please!

The crowd dies down.

MAI: Thank you David.

They smile. He gestures to the crowd now waiting for her to speak.

Thank you everyone for coming.

Maya Angelou said:

"There is no greater agony than bearing an untold story inside you."

When I began this project, I didn't really understand what I'd started. I just knew that it was something…something I had to do. No matter how hard. Or painful.

At the start of the process, I interviewed people I knew, people who wanted to share their stories with me. I was scared. I didn't know how to approach, or even talk to my own community. But as the project grew, others came forward and I realised that this was something bigger than myself. More than just my own journey.

Enter FATHER.

The people in these photographs have shared their memories with me. Their painful, fascinating, humorous memories. The stories behind these individual pictures, show us the power of memory. How it conceals and shrouds, as much as keeps things alive…

MAI falters.

Act One

SCENE ONE

Oct 1989. Epping. Lights up on the living/dining space of the Nguyen household. It is square, typical of post-war terraces coping with the overflow from London. Everything in it is old and out of fashion. Nothing matches. There is a mini shrine in the corner. A black and white photo of an old Vietnamese man and woman in traditional dress stands next to a rather large decorative statue of the Virgin Mary, some fresh flowers and satsumas. The table is set for a special dinner. There is a door leading to the kitchen. Up the stairs, two sewing machines are squeezed into a tiny box room alongside piles of textiles. There are other rooms in the house but this is indicated rather than seen.

MOTHER, 48, is dressed in her best áo dài (traditional Vietnamese dress). She's watching the news playing on the very small television whilst rearranging the table.

BBC NEWS BROADCAST: 'The communist government of East Germany tonight announced that there will be democratic elections. Today East German people have been celebrating their new freedom. They have demonstrated their loathing of the wall which has once sealed them in and they have been travelling to the West on foot, in their cars and by Rail. Thousands upon thousands of them. The West German leader Helmut Kohl has gone to West Berlin to tell the world we are one nation.'

MOTHER: You see, freedom and democracy always win. People can only suffer so much. But the poor are still poor. Like Vietnam. Those big communist bastards in still run things. So much suffering you just don't know daughter. Eh! have you chopped the salad yet?

MAI, 12, also wearing an áo dài, appears from the kitchen with a plate of salad.

MAI: Finished!

MOTHER: No English in this house. How many times do I
have to tell you.

MAI: Xong rồi mẹ.

(Finished, mother.)

MOTHER: Are we giving this to pigs to eat. Even my dead
mother couldn't swallow this.

MAI: Thì con làm lại.

(So daughter do again.)

MOTHER: There isn't time to do it again. Let me look at you.

MAI tries to get away.

MAI: Để con đi lấy camera.

(Let daughter go get the camera.)

MOTHER: In a minute. Can't a mother look at her daughter?

MAI relents.

A little care and you're almost pretty. So beautiful.
(Referring to the dress, not MAI.) Your grandmother
embroidered this for me. You children think I am difficult.
Your grandmother was a hundred times worse. Stand up
straight. What's the matter with you?

MAI: Nó chật qúa.

(It's too tight.)

MOTHER: You're fat. When I was your age I was half your size.

MAI: Con mặc áo khác được không?

(Can daughter wear something else?)

MOTHER: You are Vietnamese, so you wear a Vietnamese dress.

MAI: But we're not in Vietnam.

MOTHER: No English! Do you want a beating? This is a special day for your brother. I don't want any arguments.

MAI: Dạ.

(Yes.)

MOTHER: Show him more respect.

MAI: Dạ.

(Yes.)

MOTHER: Yes who?

MAI: Dạ mẹ

(Yes, mother.)

MOTHER: Now you can go.

MAI runs off.

And brush your hair properly. This girl! Head in the clouds!

She goes round the table re-arranging the settings till she's satisfied. Enter ANH, 23, in his graduation gown.

ANH: What's mother shouting about?

MOTHER: That girl. The older she gets, the worse she gets. If we're not careful, she'll turn rotten like an English child.

ANH: It's the age.

MOTHER: Why can't she be more like you? My son! Look how handsome you are. Who would have thought.

ANH: The gown was made to fit the English. It was the smallest one they had.

MOTHER: It's you they'll be looking at. A first class degree. In mathematics, no less. You did it, my son. You did it.

ANH: Don't mother. You'll embarrass me. Son didn't do anything.

MOTHER: Didn't do anything? You could have fallen into drink and drugs like the other boys at the camp, but you didn't. You listened to your mother. Your mother is clever, so you are clever. It's in the genes. Come here. Let me fix your tie.

He lets her fuss.

When I think about how you were without me…

ANH: Your letters kept me going.

MOTHER: Words are a way to people's hearts. Everyone has their number remember. Some are lucky, some not so lucky. And you, are lucky you have me.

ANH: Son will always try for you.

MOTHER: You are truly good, my son. Now put on that hat.

He puts it on and beams proudly.

MOTHER: Photo. Mai!

She looks in the mirror.

How about your mother? I scrub up well no? In the old days I looked like Jacquie Kennedy, now look at me. All day sitting at the sewing machine… A little round in the middle but I still have the charm. Isn't that right?

ANH: You look beautiful, mother.

MOTHER: We better get going. Where has your father got to? Probably busy getting older and clumsier. OLD MAN, TIME TO GO!

The doorbell rings.

MAI: Con mở cho!

(Daughter will open!)

MAI comes pounding down the stairs.

MOTHER: Don't run! My god. One day she's going to fall down and break her teeth.

MR DINH: Are your parents home?

MAI: Ba mẹ, chú Đinh's here.

(Mother, father, Mr Dinh's here.)

ANH takes off his hat and gown.

MOTHER: What does this man want now?

Enter MR DINH. A man in his late 30s, but looks older. He comes in carrying a bag full of textiles.

ANH: Hello Mr Dinh.

MR DINH: Anh. You look smart.

ANH: Thank you, uncle. How's your health?

MR DINH: Oh well you know, never a moments rest.

MOTHER: Mr Dinh, we weren't expecting you till Friday.

Points at the hat and gown.

MR DINH: …may I try that on?

ANH: Erm /

MR DINH: I've always wanted to see what I looked like in one of those.

ANH: It's on loan. I shouldn't /

MR DINH: Only for a moment.

He takes the hat and puts it on. MOTHER takes it off him.

MOTHER: We're running late Mr Dinh. Anh, go fetch your father. Seems like he's operating on elastic time.

Exit ANH.

MR DINH: So it's today.

MOTHER: Top of his class.

MR DINH: I've heard. The whole community's heard. You must be very proud. Shame it's not Cambridge or Oxford.

MOTHER: Mai, have you greeted Mr Dinh properly.

MAI: Chào chú, chú khỏe không?

(Hello uncle. How's your health?)

MR DINH surveys MAI.

MR DINH: I'm good, I'm good. Good girl. Still speaks Vietnamese?

MOTHER: Her Vietnamese is getting worse by the day. Soon she'll be like a dumb child.

MR DINH: As long as she understands your insults, that's all that's needed.

MOTHER: The day I can't discipline my children, is the day I die.

MR DINH: She's grown. She looks like you.

MOTHER: She's a dustbin child.

MAI: Tại sao mẹ nói vạy hoài?

(Why do you keep saying that?)

MR DINH: Your mother knows how to joke. Soon you'll be old enough to start helping your mum work.

MOTHER: I don't make my children work when they have school.

MR DINH: There's no harm in it. Isn't that right Mai?

MAI: Yes chú.

(Yes uncle.)

MOTHER: Enough, go upstairs and fetch your father.

MAI: Nhưng mà…

(But…)

MOTHER: Now.

MAI: Dạ mẹ.

(Yes mother.)

Exit MAI.

MR DINH: Your daughter has turned out very pretty.

MOTHER: What can we do for you Mr Dinh?

MR DINH puts down a bag of textiles in front of MOTHER.

MR DINH: Quality control. New rules. I'm really sorry but I have to ask you to unpick them and start again. Just the lining. The hems. They're a little snaky.

He makes a squiggly line with his finger.

MOTHER: Snaky?

MR DINH: Like I said, it's quality control. There's more competition. Things are being shipped abroad. We have to be vigilant.

MOTHER: Show me. Show me these hems.

MR DINH: Look for yourself.

She riffles through the bags.

MOTHER: I can't see anything wrong.

MR DINH: Look closer.

MOTHER: There's nothing wrong with them. You must have made a mistake.

MR DINH comes over, he picks out a skirt and shows MOTHER the mistake in one of them.

MR DINH: Old woman. Why do you have to question me?

MOTHER: What, this? There's nothing there. You can barely see this.

MR DINH: There!

MOTHER: Are you crazy old man. It's the way the pattern is cut, that's not our fault.

MR DINH: Look, I know this isn't usual but I really need these done by tomorrow.

MOTHER: What are you trying to do? Break our backs? We won't be able to get all these done by tomorrow.

MR DINH: Otherwise the work will get shipped to someone else.

MOTHER: I know you have more power than that you clumsy fool! You're doing this to spite me.

MR DINH: Old woman. You can think what you like, but I still need them done. If you want to carry on having the 50p skirts/

MOTHER: Are you threatening me?

MR DINH: Lots of people need work. We all need to make a living? Anh's going to make his millions. That's what you've been shouting about all over the community. Not everyone's as lucky.

Enter FATHER looking dishevelled in his suit. He has bits of thread all over it. He greets MR DINH warmly.

FATHER: Mr Dinh. How's your health?

MOTHER: Old man, come and sort this out.

She starts picking the thread off his suit.

MR DINH: Mr Nguyen. Good good./ And yours?

FATHER bats her away.

FATHER: Enough woman. Good. Yes.

MOTHER: This crazy man expects us to re-do all these skirts by tomorrow. Old man, talk to him.

FATHER: What's the problem Mr Dinh? This woman being difficult again.

MR DINH: I'm sorry old man, my hands are tied. You know it's nothing personal. The hems need fixing.

FATHER: If you say they need to be done/ we'll fix them.

MOTHER: It's only a little mistake. They don't need doing again.

MR DINH: I was just explaining to the old woman –

MOTHER: He's threatening to stop our 50p skirts.

MR DINH: You understand old man, I have to keep everyone happy. The clients are getting more demanding. If they're not perfect they get sent back. I'm under pressure from all the working families. You know how all these women are. They talk my ears off.

FATHER: I do. I have one right here. You know we never let you down.

MR DINH: If you can get them done, I'll keep your 50p skirts going.

FATHER: That's very kind of you. Thank you. Thank you.

MR DINH: You know I respect you.

FATHER: That's enough. That's enough.

MR DINH: I know you have a daughter to look after.

FATHER: Yes growing up fast. And your son?

MR DINH: Making me proud. Eh, how about promising them to each other?

MOTHER: Mai's studying to be a doctor, she's got no time for boys.

FATHER: Old woman.

MR DINH: He's making good money. She can stay at home. Look after the children. Good money and experience old man. That's what you get from starting work early. Nothing you can learn in books.

FATHER: That's right old man, you speak the truth.

MOTHER: She's stubborn and disobedient, you wouldn't want her.

FATHER: She would be lucky to have him. We should talk about it over dinner.

MR DINH spies the laid out dinner table.

MR DINH: Crab noodle soup? *(Bún Riêu)*

FATHER: Would you like a bowl?

MR DINH: Reminds me of home.

FATHER: This woman can make a few bones turn into something out of this world.

MOTHER: It's not ready yet.

FATHER: I had some this morning. It tasted fine.

MOTHER: You were in a labour camp for years. Ate nothing but sweet potato, what do you know.

MR DINH: It's okay, it's okay, I better get going anyway. Got to do the rounds.

FATHER: Yes, of course you do. You're a busy man.

MR DINH: Good to see you old man. I'll pick these up tomorrow. Look after yourself. I'll let myself out.

Exit MR DINH. FATHER pulls out the skirts. He takes out a pair of sewing clippers from his pocket and starts work straight away.

MOTHER: We shouldn't have let her do those hems. I knew this would happen. This girl. Can never do anything properly.

FATHER: You needed the rest.

MOTHER: I should have done it myself. Now we've created twice as much work. Mai!/

FATHER: Old woman. Leave her. It wasn't her fault.

MOTHER: Wasn't her… Daydreaming is what she was doing.

FATHER: I'll deal with this.

22

MOTHER: And you old man. You don't help. How can you talk to that man? He's worse than Viet Cong.

FATHER: What's the matter now?

MOTHER: Just because we're a little better educated, he's finding ways to drag us down. Evil communist pig. I'm not going to bow down to him.

FATHER: Old woman, don't make a fuss. I will fix it.

MOTHER: Let's see, let's see who comes up top. 10 years from now he won't be worthy to lick the dirt off my son's shoe. And you. Are you crazy? Even contemplating marrying our daughter to that peasant family. There are times, you're so stupid I can't even look at you.

FATHER: You have to flatter people a little to get what you want.

MOTHER: You want me to sweet talk that low life? Easy for you to do but I'm not so easily bullied.

FATHER: Old woman, hold that tongue of yours. One day you're going to go too far.

MOTHER: Who's going to stop me? We're in the land of the free, I can say what I want.

FATHER: Yes, you always have something to say.

MOTHER: Better to have something to say than being dumb and stupid.

FATHER: We'll get the 50p skirts next week.

MOTHER: Jesus Christ. He knows we can't keep this up. It'll give him the excuse to give the good stuff to someone else. We'll end up with the 10p trousers! We'll have to do 16 hour days just to make a tiny bit of money. We are not

23

missing Anh's graduation because of him. I'd rather clean toilets.

FATHER: It's just a piece of paper. I'll stay at home and sort this.

MOTHER: Mai! Anh! Get down here. It's time to go!

Enter ANH followed by MAI with a disposable camera in her hand.

ANH: What's happening now?

MOTHER: Nothing.

FATHER: You lot go, I'm staying here.

ANH sees the mess on the floor.

MOTHER: Leave your father. If he wants to lick Mr Dinh's arse, let him. Mai, upstairs. We need to fix your hair. How do you manage to still look so messy.

MAI: Nếu ba ở nhà, con ở nhà được không?

(If father stay house, daughter stay at home okay?)

MOTHER: You're not staying at home. Your father can do what he likes.

MOTHER and MAI leave.

ANH: Is father really doing this now?

FATHER: It was our mistake. We can't say no to our mistake. If something needs to be done.

ANH: Today is for mother, not me.

FATHER: Today is just another day.

ANH: This was a chance for all of us to get out of the house.

FATHER: You think you're the man now?

ANH: Fine. Then father stay behind.

FATHER: Watch that tone of yours.

ANH: Son will get a job soon. Father won't have to sew any longer.

FATHER: When you find that job, I'll stop. Till then, I'll sew.

MOTHER: Anh let's go, we're ready.

MAI comes in after MOTHER in pigtails.

ANH: I didn't say anything.

She snaps a picture of him in return.

Hey!

MAI: One for the photo album.

MOTHER: Mai! Don't waste film. Old man, make sure you work in the light or you'll go blind.

ANH: –

MOTHER: Anh, leave your father.

ANH exits, leaving FATHER alone.

FATHER makes the sign of the cross and starts praying under his breath.

MAI lagging behind and snaps a photo of FATHER unpicking the skirts unnoticed by him.

She leaves.

He prays.

These photos might go in the exhibition.

SCENE TWO

It's March 1991. There is now a posed picture of ANH in his graduation gown on the wall. FATHER and MR DINH are drinking beer, eating beer food (salted squid, rare beef and pigs intestines) and playing cards in the living room with the TV in the background. MOTHER and MAI are working in the sewing room, overturning the last of the skirts and putting them in the bag.

BBC NEWS BROADCAST: 'President Bush has just said the air war against Iraq will continue for a while. The Iraqi's say that more than six thousand civilians have been killed in the Gulf war, but the allies have again insisted that bombing has avoided civilian targets. And here fifty firms a day are going bankrupt as the recession deepens.'

FATHER: Queen, King, Ace! I win!

MR DINH: Fuck your mother, that was unlucky.

FATHER: Better luck next time.

MAI: Mẹ.

(Mother.)

MOTHER: What?

MAI: Chừng nào con finish, con go cinema được không?

(After daughter finish this, daughter go to cinema, is it okay?)

MR DINH: When will those Americans learn.

MOTHER: You have to study.

FATHER: Their promise of freedom is a seductive thing.

MAI: Nhưng mà hôm nay là Saturday.

(But it's Saturday.)

FATHER: Makes them think they're Gods.

26

MOTHER: I don't care.

MR DINH: You feel free old man?

MAI: Mẹ…

(Mother…)

FATHER: Being married to my woman is more of a prison than re-education camp.

MR DINH: Ha!

MAI: All Anh did was study and look where it got him. *(Under her breath.)*

FATHER: What does freedom mean anyway.

MOTHER: If you go near ink, you'll stain. If you go near light, you'll be bright.

MR DINH: For me, enough money to control my destiny.

MOTHER: All I do is work till the skin is falling off my bones, and this is what I get. An ungrateful rotten daughter.

FATHER: You'll be chasing that forever.

MAI: Con gái bà Lê is only 13 but bà Lê cho her go out hoài. Con 14! mà mẹ never let me go anywhere.

(Daughter of Mrs Le is only thirteen but Mrs Le let her go out all the time. Daughter fourteen, but mother never let me go anywhere.)

MR DINH: Both our governments lied to us.

MOTHER: Old woman Le's daughter is different. You think because you're 14 you can do what you want? The Le family are peasants. Happy as long as they have food to eat.

MR DINH: They promised life would be better after we got independence, but we just starved.

MOTHER: In Vietnam, you wouldn't even be in the same neighbourhood. Here, you're forced to be friends.

MR DINH: No room to breathe without a permit.

MAI: *(Under her breath.)* At least they're happy.

MR DINH: Lucky I had the entrepreneurial spirit to escape.

MOTHER: You want to be like the Le girl? Free to do as you please? Then go. It would be easy to let you run free.

FATHER: A few drinks and you start with the politics.

MOTHER: The body wants to play and have a good time. You need to fight against it. If I went with how I felt, you wouldn't be here.

FATHER: What's past is past.

MOTHER: It feels good to lie down and relax. But you do that, life will trample all over you. You have to be ready.

FATHER: Another game?

MAI: What for?

MOTHER: What did I say about speaking English in this house.

MR DINH: I don't want to play you anymore. It's too risky.

MAI: Mà ba said/

   But father said/

FATHER: That's because I have Jesus Christ on my side. Whereas you've only got your dead ancestors.

MOTHER: I don't care what your father says. What I say goes.

MR DINH: My ancestors beat your God any day.

MOTHER: All he cares about is eating, drinking, and going to church. Too busy repenting his sins. It's only the mother that cares. It's always the mother.

FATHER: Prove it.

MR DINH: Okay.

MOTHER: You think you know daughter, but you don't.
I have been running away from bombs and death since I was five years old.

MR DINH: Look old man…

MOTHER: My parents suffered.

MR DINH: You know I wouldn't be doing this if I could help it.

MOTHER: They died without any of their children by their side.

FATHER: We won't starve. Don't worry.

MOTHER: God gave me the talent to calculate my way to freedom. He's going to show us a way out of this.

MR DINH: I'm not sure your old woman will see it that way.

FATHER: That woman is still fighting a war in her head. It's her against the world.

MOTHER: The English, they treat us with kindness when we are helpless. As soon as we succeed a little, they show their true colours.

MR DINH: Sometimes I envy you.

FATHER: What is there to envy.

MOTHER: You don't see Mai. Your brother suffers.

MR DINH: You have a strong woman.

FATHER: Hard as rock.

MOTHER: This girl! Are you listening?

MAI: Có! Con có nghe.

(Yes! Daughter is listening.)

MR DINH: All my wife seems to be able to do is spend my money. She can't cook. Not like this. And a woman should be able to cook.

FATHER: Ah, it's your stomach talking.

MR DINH: Beer and salty snacks. Where the hell does she get the ingredients?

FATHER: She's always been resourceful.

MR DINH: In my house, I have to carry all the burden.

FATHER: We can swap if you like.

MR DINH: Ha ha ha… be careful, I might take you up on that.

MOTHER: Have you nearly finished?

FATHER: You really have had too much to drink.

MOTHER: Start folding them away.

MAI and MOTHER fold.

MR DINH: Eh, do you miss it?

FATHER: Miss what?

MR DINH: Home.

FATHER: What is there to miss?

MR DINH: The smells. The sticky weather. Fresh jack fruit everywhere you go. When I left, I thought I'd never look back. As time goes by, all I think about is going back.

FATHER: You're longing for something that's not possible.

MR DINH: I still have family there. In-laws and a hundred cousins drowning my finances. As soon as I can, I'm going back. Make enough money and go live like a King.

FATHER: The Vietnam I know is dead.

MR DINH: Old man, don't be like that. The war is over.

FATHER: For you maybe. But for me, there will always be enemies.

MR DINH: The Americans underestimated the power of the North. It was clear who was going to win.

FATHER: I told you no politics! The communists were pure evil. You didn't see the things I saw. If you did, making money would not be the top of your list.

MR DINH: I didn't mean to bring up bad memories. I'm trying to say, North, South. It doesn't matter. We're all together now.

FATHER: My men died in that war and are being forgotten. At least in America there's a community who remember. I'm stuck, in Epping, where we all just disappear.

MR DINH: I tell you now, old man. No one is free in America. Especially the immigrants. Especially us. No one cares for the Asians.

FATHER: Enough.

MR DINH: Old man, tell me you're not offended. I know you're a northerner at heart.

FATHER: What is that supposed / to mean?

MR DINH: / That's why we're friends no?

FATHER: Before '54, I was just Vietnamese. Then they forced us Catholics out, drew a line, now it's northerners and southerners.

MR DINH: Religion and war go hand in hand. Everyone knows that. It was a necessary step to independence.

FATHER: And look where it's got us. We both live in a place where all the colour has been drained out. Wet and miserable.

MR DINH: What's your favourite food?

FATHER: What?

MR DINH: Just say it.

FATHER: Salty stewed fish *(Cá Kho)* of course.

MR DINH: Then you're a child of Ha Noi my friend.

FATHER: Ha ha ha…you speak the truth. You speak the truth.

MR DINH: See. I really think we should join forces.

FATHER: That again.

MR DINH: Bridge that gap.

FATHER: You really want my woman as your in law?

MR DINH: My son won't stop pestering me. Mai's put some spell over him. From afar I mean. I'm not implying anything. She is a rare beauty. You know Tuan, he's as soft as a bear.

FATHER: I know. The boy wouldn't hurt a fly. That's what I'm worried about.

MR DINH: He's also strong as an ox. You won't do better.

FATHER: When the time comes / we'll talk.

MR DINH: The time is now. Do you not see the things they show on television. All lipstick and short skirts.

FATHER: Mai isn't like that.

MR DINH: Of course not, old man. I'm just saying.

FATHER: Maybe you are right. Maybe it is time.

MR DINH: Really?

FATHER: You have my word.

MR DINH: Old man. You won't regret this.

FATHER slaps a winning hand down.

FATHER: I win again.

MR DINH: Fuck your mother!

Enter MOTHER and MAI with the bag of textiles.

MOTHER: That's it.

MR DINH: Ah perfect timing. I was just about to leave. Thank you for the drinking snacks. They were delicious.

MOTHER: It's all there. You don't have to check it.

MR DINH: Eh Mai, me and your father were just discussing you.

MOTHER: Mai, go upstairs. It's time for bed.

MAI: Mà it's vẫn early mẹ.

(It's still early, mother.)

MOTHER: Then practice your piano. I want you to be able to play Mother's Love at my funeral.

MAI: Mà mẹ đâu có chết đâu.

(But you're not going to die.)

MOTHER: How do you know? I could die tomorrow and none of you children would care. See Mr Dinh, what a disobedient child I have.

MR DINH: They're all like this at this age.

FATHER: Do what your mother says.

MAI: Dạ ba.

(Yes, father.)

MAI leaves. Stomping up the stairs. A minute later loud angry piano playing of Lòng Mẹ can be heard.

MOTHER: Mai!

The playing softens.

MR DINH: Spirited isn't she. Here.

MR DINH hands her a brown paper envelope.

There's a little extra in there. I hear Anh still hasn't found a job yet. How long has it been? A year?

MOTHER: We don't need your charity.

She counts the money.

MR DINH: I'm sorry it's ending like this, but that's economics for you. I warned you that China were undercutting our prices. Though there might be work in my new restaurant if you're interested. It's doing very well. We've got them queuing up. Can't get enough of that Chilli and Black Bean sauce.

MOTHER: Why would I work in a Chinese restaurant. I'm not Chinese.

MR DINH: They've been running successful restaurants for years.

MOTHER: They're also evil communists.

MR DINH: I know what a good cook you are.

MOTHER: I'm not for hire.

MR DINH: Well maybe Anh then.

MOTHER: He's got a job. A good one.

They both know this isn't true.

MR DINH: I'm only going to offer once.

MOTHER: You're very kind but we're fine.

MR DINH: You need to learn to accept a hand out now and then, you know, woman.

MOTHER: There are people able to do that, we're not one of them.

MR DINH: Old man let's do this again.

FATHER: You know where I am.

MOTHER: Goodbye Mr Dinh.

MR DINH: Take care, old woman.

Exit MR DINH. ANH appears on the stairs.

MOTHER: As if Anh would work in his restaurant, just so he can gloat at us every day.

FATHER: Old woman.

MOTHER: What?

FATHER: Why do you always have to provoke people.

MOTHER: I don't know how you can mix with those people. Those people aren't to be trus/

He sits and starts playing solitaire.

Old man, you are unbelievable. We're in a recession.

FATHER: We can't do anything about that.

MOTHER: We need to come up with a plan.

FATHER: Mmmm.

MOTHER: You want us to live off benefits for the rest of our lives? We have two hands two feet, we can work, we can make money. If Mr Dinh can do it why can't we.

FATHER: Be quiet, woman.

MOTHER: We'll have to get more cleaning jobs till Anh finds something.

FATHER: *If* he finds something.

MOTHER: Have faith in your son.

FATHER: You filled his head with dreams.

MOTHER: You've lost all self-belief, you want everyone else to be like you.

FATHER: I have a headache. I'm going to bed.

He stands. ANH disappears from the stairs and heads out the door.

MOTHER: What about Mai?

FATHER: She's a girl. She can marry.

MOTHER: And be taken care of by a man? Like you take care of me?

FATHER: Tuan is a nice boy. I've set it. I don't want to talk anymore.

MOTHER: That drowned chicken of a boy is not coming near / my daughter.

FATHER: / I've given my word. I never go against my word.

MOTHER: Only to keep up appearances.

FATHER: They will look after her.

MOTHER: How do you know? You never look beyond today. I know. I can see.

FATHER: I'm going to bed.

Exit FATHER.

MOTHER: Is that it? No more arguing?

There's no answer

Fine. Sleep. Disappear. Leave me to worry about our family on my own like you always do.

As soon as he's out of sight MOTHER opens up one of the seat cushions and pulls out a wad of cash. She takes out the cash from the envelope and adds it to the pile. She counts the money.

As she counts…

Lights up on MR DINH and ANH, who has caught up with him outside the house.

ANH: Mr Dinh, let me help you with those bags.

MR DINH: Anh? Where did you spring from?

ANH: I heard about your restaurant opening. I wanted to congratulate uncle.

MR DINH: That's very kind.

ANH: How's business?

MR DINH: I might not have a university education but I don't do too badly.

ANH: I wondered if/

MR DINH: Your mother must be very proud of you.

ANH: Yes she is.

MR DINH: It breaks my heart to see them scrub toilets to live. I know how hard it is out there. You don't have to pretend with me.

ANH: Actually uncle, that's the real reason I came out here.

MR DINH: Oh?

ANH: I think I…maybe I could come and work for you. As a business adviser?

MR DINH: A what adviser?

ANH: I have a business idea. I was hoping I could come to the/

MR DINH: What's the idea?

ANH: Maybe I could come to the restaurant and/

MR DINH: I'd like to hear it.

ANH: Now?

MR DINH: There's no time like the present. Don't you want to?

ANH: Yes but…

MR DINH: Say it. Don't be shy.

ANH: Okay uncle.

MR DINH: I'm listening.

ANH: I've worked out a business plan. With the right investment and accounting, you could expand. The English, they're different to us. They want to beat each other. We are born to be like family. If uncle makes

38

full use of our workers, uncle could have a chain of restaurants.

MR DINH: A chain?

ANH: All over the town. Like MacDonald's.

MR DINH: MacDonald's?

ANH: Well not at first. But we can build it up. Make it strong and then/

MR DINH: That big?

ANH: You can have two, then three, then MacDonald's.

MR DINH: I will talk to Tuan about it.

ANH: I am sure he is too busy. I can help with all of that. The legal stuff, everything.

MR DINH: He takes care of that.

ANH: I mean no offence uncle Dinh, it's just that neither of you are trained in accounts. There are people who will take advantage. I could help with that.

MR DINH: How much would I have to pay for this service of yours?

ANH: Uncle is an old family friend... I would work for 10,000 a year.

MR DINH: Is that what you think that piece of paper of yours is worth?

ANH: That's less than the going rate.

MR DINH: Not here it's not.

ANH: I can go a little lower... 8,000.

MR DINH: As much as I would love to help you Anh, the world does not work on good intentions.

ANH: I'm offering you something good.

MR DINH: We're almost family. But as it is, the business is doing fine.

ANH: 5,000, my final offer.

MR DINH: Does your mother know you're here?

ANH: I don't need her permission.

MR DINH: Are you sure?

ANH: I'm my own man. The man of the house. I need to… I need to work.

MR DINH: I understand.

Pause.

MR DINH: We do have an opening. We need someone with good English who can handle working with the public. It's a tough job. You need to start from the bottom. Get your hands dirty.

ANH: Are you asking me to be a waiter?

MR DINH: I'm not a charity.

ANH: But I can do so much more for you than–

MR DINH: I care for you, so I don't want to give you false hope. You know me. I give it to you straight. A job doesn't go unfilled for very long.

He starts to leave.

ANH: No…

MR DINH: No what?

ANH: …I'll take it.

MR DINH: Well…okay then. Tomorrow morning. 11 a.m.
The boy will show you what to do.

ANH: Yes uncle.

MR DINH: You're welcome. And Anh, your father's the man
of the house. Don't you forget that.

Lights dim on ANH and MR DINH.

*MOTHER puts things back carefully. Turning to the shrine, she kneels
down and speaks to the photos.*

MOTHER: Mother. Father. It's times like this miss you more
than ever. I feel so alone.

This old man, each day he fades away. Seeing Anh in
pain…My tears fall like rain. And Mai…she's becoming a
stranger to me. Sometimes I don't know if I can fight any
more.

*She turns to the statue of Mary, takes out her rosary and does the
sign of the cross.*

Dear Jesus son of God, you sacrificed your life for us, your
children. Give me the strength to sacrifice myself for mine.
Help me raise myself up, raise myself up…

She starts saying the Lord's prayer, beginning the rosary.

Lights fade, leaving a spotlight on MOTHER.

*The sound of MOTHER's praying becomes more audible taken over
by the faint sound of helicopters.*

SCENE THREE

Later that evening. 2 a.m. Everyone is asleep. MAI comes creeping in from the kitchen with a plate of food and a glass of water, she is fully dressed and has been out. FATHER walks into the living room. Though his eyes are open his expression is dim and glazed over. MAI freezes when she sees him but he just carries on. He is sleepwalking. He proceeds to pace in a repetitive fashion marking out a square on the floor, each side four steps long. He does this repeatedly mumbling under his breath... MAI stares, fascinated.

FATHER: I confess...I did it confess...please...please...stop... no more...no more...God forgive me...forgive me...I confess...I did it...please...please...stop...no more...no more...please...God forgive me...

MAI cautiously approaches.

FATHER: I confess...I did it confess...please...

MAI approaches her FATHER. She inadvertently knocks over the statue of the Virgin Mary.

FATHER: What...what's happening?

MAI: Ba?

(Father?)

FATHER: What–

MAI: It's okay, it's–

FATHER: Who's there?

MAI: Con đay nè

(It's daughter here.)

FATHER: Who's there?

42

MAI: Con đay–

(I'm here–)

FATHER: Daughter?

MAI: It's me, con, Mai.

FATHER: Mai? Mai. Mai. Good daughter.

MAI: Ba có sao không?

(Father okay?)

FATHER: Mmm. Mmm…

MAI: Ba/

(Father/)

FATHER: What time is it?

MAI: Tối rồi ba.

(Nighttime, father.)

FATHER: Nighttime? Where are we?

MAI: Mình ở nhà ba. Mình ở nhà.

(We're at home father. We're at home.)

FATHER: Home. Where is home? What time is it?

MAI: Ba mới hỏi con.

(Father just ask daughter.)

FATHER: Did I?

MAI: Ba… Con không biết nói…

(Father… Daughter don't know how say…)

FATHER: Where are we?

MAI: Con không biết…how to say…

(Father…daughter don't know how to say.)

FATHER: We're downstairs.

MAI: Ba was *sleepwalking*.

(Father was sleepwalking.)

FATHER: **Sleepwalking***?*

MAI: Dạ. Ba ngủ but ba vẫn walking.

(Yes. Father was sleeping but father still walking.)

He turns to look at the clock and stumbles. MAI helps him to sit.

MAI: Ba.

(Father.)

FATHER: It's okay, I'm okay. I'm just a little tired.

MAI: Ba làm việc nhiều quá that's why. Nè, uống nước đi.

(Because father work too much that's why. Here, have some water.)

She picks up the water to give to him. Suddenly violent. He knocks it out of her hand.

FATHER: I told you. Don't fuss. It's nothing.

She picks up the glass and uses her scarf to soak up the water.

You're a good child. I'm overtired that's all.

He sees what she is wearing.

Why are you dressed like that?

MAI: Con…

(Daughter…)

FATHER: Where have you been daughter? Answer me. Have you been out with b–

MAI: Không boys! Con không đi chơi với boys!

(No boys! Daughter no go play with boys!)

FATHER: Then what have you been up to? Does your mother know?

MAI: Ba đừng nói cho mẹ biết. Xin đừng nói…con…con…

(Father don't speak mother know. Please don't speak… daughter…daughter…)

FATHER: Speak in English if you can't say it.

MAI: Con chơi với friends, that's all. Con sorry ba. Con promise. I just want to go out sometimes. Con của bác Lê goes out all the time, mà mẹ never lets con go out. Ba đi ask if ba không believe me. Mẹ just wants con to stay at home and study. Like I'm in a prison or something.

FATHER: Your mother loves you that's why she does what she does.

MAI: Other people think nhà mình … con không biết nói … stuck up. Họ nghĩ rằng con something wrong. Con don't want người ta think that. If I don't go out, I don't have friends…I don't fit in anywhere…

FATHER: Why do you care what other people think. Remember the captive buffalo hates the free buffalo.

MAI: Ba nói gì. Con don't understand.

(What father saying? Daughter doesn't understand.)

FATHER: You can always be free, up here. *(He points to his temple.)* They can't take that away from you. They can't take that away from you.

Pause.

MAI: Ba?

   (Father?)

FATHER: You shouldn't be out so late. What if something happened to you?

MAI: Con okay. Ba nhìn đây. Con okay.

   (Daughter okay. Father look here. Daughter okay.)

   Pause.

   Ba có sao không?

   (Father okay?)

FATHER: Promise me you won't sneak out again.

MAI: Con hứa

   (Daughter promise.)

   We see MOTHER on the stairs listening.

FATHER: Promise me.

MAI: Con hứa

   (Daughter promise.)

FATHER: Remember.

MAI: Con nhớ. Ba, has this happened before?

   (Daughter remember. Father, has this happened before?)

FATHER: Let's forget about tonight.

MAI: Ba.

FATHER: It's nothing.

MAI: –

FATHER: I won't tell your mother.

MAI: Cám ơn ba.

(Thank you father.)

FATHER: It'll be our secret.

MAI: Dạ ba

(Yes father.)

FATHER: **Remember**.

MAI: Con remember.

FATHER: Good daughter.

SCENE FOUR

Summer 1992. It's late. MAI in her pyjamas on the phone.

MAI: I like can't right now…I just can't…of course I want to see you, it's not that. It's not as easy for me is it.

ANH enters. He's been drinking.

ANH: Who are you talking to?

MAI: Anh man! You scared me!

He grabs the phone off her. In a mock Vietnamese accent.

ANH: **Who this? This Mai's father. If you call here again, I kill you. I chop your balls off, you hear me!**

He laughs. Slams down the phone.

MAI: What did you do that for?

ANH: *(Mimicking her.)* What did you do that for?

MAI: What's the matter with you?

ANH: Does mum know what you're up to?

MAI: Up to what?

ANH: Don't act innocent.

MAI: You're drunk init.

ANH: Stop saying init. Trying to be something you're not.

MAI: Oh get lost.

ANH: Piggy!/ Get me something to eat.

MAI: Keep your voice down will you.

ANH: Yes, don't want to wake up the oldies do we? Well go on then, chop chop.

MAI: God I hate you.

He goes and hunts for a drink in the cabinet and finds a bottle of Remy Martin. MAI comes back with some cold meat. He offers her his drink.

Drink?

She goes to grab it and he snatches it away.

Don't be stupid.

MAI: You're horrible you are.

He gestures her to take the bottle. She drinks, coughs.

ANH: Good eh.

MAI: Yeah great.

ANH: You'll learn.

MAI: You're not like, going to tell on me are you?

ANH: Not if you don't tell on me.

MAI: Why? What have you done.

ANH fishes out a little Lomo camera from his coat pocket and throws it at her.

MAI: Is this for me?

ANH: –

MAI: Are you serious? Oh my god. Thank you thank you thank you.

She knocks his drink

ANH: Watch it?!

MAI: Wait. You can't afford this.

ANH: Happy Birthday.

MAI: This is like the nicest thing you've ever done for me.

ANH: Don't worry about it.

MAI: No seriously...

ANH: Just couldn't stand to hear you go on about it anymore. Just don't tell mum. Say you got borrowed it from school or something. She'll believe that.

MAI: Thanks, big brother.

ANH: Yeah well don't get used to it.

She gives him a hug after some hesitation then starts to leave.

ANH: Where do you think you're going?

MAI: To try it out.

ANH: Sit and talk to me.

MAI: You what?

ANH: Sit.

MAI: You want me, to sit, and talk, to you?

ANH: Why. Something wrong with that?

MAI: Well…yeah.

ANH: I bet you'd have time to talk to your boyfriend.

MAI: Shut up. He's not my boyfriend.

ANH: Gotcha!

MAI: That's it. I'm going.

She moves to go.

ANH: No! Stay. I was only teasing. Keep me company for a while.

MAI: What do you want to talk about?

ANH: I don't know. Anything you want.

They sit. Long pause. He eats.

ANH: Want some?

MAI: You stink of cigarettes.

Long pause. He eats.

MAI: Okay, can I ask you a question?

ANH: Depends what it is?

MAI: You know, dad, being in the war and stuff. Do you think it's like, affected him. You know, mentally?

ANH: That's a stupid question.

MAI: You were…you know… there.

ANH: I was younger than you.

MAI: I thought you might/

ANH: One minute I was kicking a shuttlecock in the back garden, the next minute I'm on a fishing vessel.

MAI: What was it like?

ANH: What?

MAI: The journey.

ANH: I haven't thought about it in years.

MAI: You don't have to if…

ANH: It was tiny.

MAI: –

ANH: I remember thinking this might not float. We were squashed in like sardines. Just floating, waiting for God to take us where we needed to go. That was the hardest bit. And the hunger, thirst… fear of pirates. I was scared shitless … I suppose it was an adventure. Now, now it feels like I'm drowning.

MAI: –

ANH: Have you ever seen a dead body Mai?

MAI shakes her head.

ANH: I have. Dead bodies on every street left to swell up and stink. You don't want to talk about it. You want to forget. I'm a bad brother.

She stands up and realises MOTHER is there in her nightgown, looking tired and drawn. MOTHER enters takes the drink off ANH.

MOTHER: Mai, go upstairs. I want to talk to your brother.

MAI: Nhưng mà/

(But/)

MOTHER: Go! Now!

MAI leaves. MOTHER starts to tidy up.

You shouldn't drink like that in front of your sister. One leads to another and another. It's bad for the stomach.

ANH: I'm not addicted mother.

MOTHER: No one's addicted till it's too late.

ANH: I wish mother wouldn't fuss over me. I know what I'm doing.

MOTHER: You two think you're so clever.

ANH: What's wrong now.

MOTHER: You think your mother is stupid? I know where you've been. The tongues have been waggling all over the community. All my effort, all my hard work, and he goes and he lies to me.

ANH: Enough mother. Don't say anything more.

MOTHER: At first I was angry, but then I kept my mouth shut. I wanted to see what would happen. How long you would last. But look at you. Look at what it's doing to you. You are better than this.

ANH: Please mother. You don't know what it's like out there. What it's like for me.

MOTHER: I understand what the world can do for you. Me and your father we're old. We don't speak the language. Don't understand the culture. But you were given an education. A roof over your head. You have to believe in yourself. You are destined for bigger things.

ANH: Son wish mother would stop saying that.

MOTHER: I know. A mother knows.

ANH: How do you know? You keep thinking that we're better than the rest. We're not. There's nothing out there for us Vietnamese. You always think...you sit there, you think that if I study hard, work hard, I can do anything. But it's not like that mum. The English, they don't think that.

MOTHER: You think there is nothing out there for us? You think that you are failing because you are Vietnamese?

ANH: That's right.

MOTHER: It is not because you are Vietnamese. It is because you are giving up.

ANH: You told me to study, I studied. You told me to go to university, I went. I came out, did the interviews, and there's nothing for me. They look at me, look at my face and they don't want to give me a job. Why would they give the job to a small man they don't understand.

MOTHER: This their country. But you need to be stronger and smarter than the white man. You children come to a bump in the road and you think it's a mountain. When things are down they have to go up. Do you think I am blind to all the things you're saying. I know. I see. I hear. But I keep it inside. Heavens I suffer. How I suffer for you children.

ANH: The whole world is suffering

MOTHER: You're exactly like your father.

ANH: I'm nothing like him.

MOTHER: So prove it to me. Prove to me what you're made of.

She starts opening the cushions.

53

MOTHER: This is what we're going to do. You think I don't know what is out there. I do. Look, look at this.

ANH: Mother, how much is here?

MOTHER: There will be more.

ANH: Where did all this come from?

MOTHER: I've been calculating every day. I think about the future all the time. We take this money. We take this money and we open our own restaurant.

ANH: A restaurant?

MOTHER: Listen to me. Stupid Mr Dinh is following the Chinese like a sheep. But with this money, and a little more, we can do something better. Me and you.

ANH: I don't understand.

MOTHER: We start small. I know someone who can rent us a space. We open something completely new. Something different. I've been reading in the paper. About the Japanese. About the Chinese. About the Thai people making a lot of money from their food. Our food is fresh, it's new. We can make a lot of money.

ANH: A Vietnamese restaurant?

MOTHER: In Vietnam, you don't know son, it was a different world back then. I ate in the finest restaurants. Food from the north all the way to the south. Food influenced by the French. Butter and fish sauce. People wouldn't think it goes together, but it does. Butter and fish sauce. We do it together.

ANH: But we don't know anything about...

MOTHER: No one knows before they begin. You're already working for Mr Dinh. I want you to look. Listen. Learn what there is to learn. Use Mr Dinh for what he has. It's better to be the head of a chicken, than a tail of a bull.

ANH: Our own restaurant.

MOTHER: People need to eat, that's one thing you can count on. What have we got to lose my son? What is there to lose?

END OF ACT ONE

Act Two

1995. Evening. The Nguyen house. The furniture has been updated and there is new wallpaper on the walls. A bigger tv has replaced the old one, but the shrine still stays the same. The space occupied by the sewing machines has been replaced by boxes of dry food etc. for the new restaurant. The tv is on. MAI and DAVID are lying on the living room floor sharing a spliff. There is a book open on the shellshocked image of an American soldier by Don McCullin.

BBC NEWS BROADCAST: 'It has officials say been the biggest and fastest flight of humanity the UN has witnessed in nearly fifty years. 10s of 1000s of refugees pouring out of the country. East to Tanzania and here north to Uganda. Altogether it's estimated that more than a million people have been forced from their homes but a campaign of butchery that shows no signs of ending...'

DAVID turns it off.

MAI: Hey! I was listening to that.

DAVID: What for?

MAI: Things are happening in the world.

DAVID: You can't save humanity, Mai.

MAI: Wow.

DAVID: Hey what do you think he's thinking?

MAI: Don't know.

DAVID: He looks...

MAI: I don't think he has a thought in his mind...

DAVID: …smashed. Completely smashed.

MAI: No…he has thought, but it's not thought, you know what I mean?

DAVID: Yeah.

MAI: Stuff you can't put into words. You can feel it but you can't really express it. That's why I love pictures. It's stuff you can't put into words.

DAVID: I wonder what it's like.

MAI: What?

DAVID: You know, to see that shit. See people being blown up and shit.

MAI: Look at his face. What do you think?

DAVID: I think he looks stoned.

MAI: Like numb.

DAVID: Yeah numb.

MAI: Yeah numb.

He starts to laugh

MAI: What are you laughing at?

DAVID: Nothing.

MAI: Are you laughing at me?

DAVID: No. Yes. A little bit.

MAI: It's not funny. Look at him. It's not pretend. We don't even know what happened to him. He could be a zombie in some mental hospital, or dead if he's lucky. Or he could be living a life where he's like this but on the inside forever but no one gives a shit because they're too fucking busy getting on with their own lives.

DAVID: Alright Mai. Chill out. I didn't mean anything by it.

MAI: I'm just saying. They don't teach us this stuff at school.

DAVID: I'm not sure it's something you can teach.

MAI: What?

DAVID: I don't think you can teach this stuff.

MAI: The war memorial in Washington has something like 60 thousand American names on it, but there are something like 5 times that amount of South Vietnamese who fought and died next to them, but none of them are on it.

DAVID: I love it when you get like this.

MAI: I mean, what do you do with that kind of info?

DAVID: You let it feed your art. Take it from the black man.

MAI: You're not a black man, you're a black boy. And anyway it's different. You're cool and I'm not.

DAVID: What did I just hear?

MAI: You walk down the street and everyone, like everyone stops to say hello. Everyone around here knows you. This your tribe.

DAVID: Everyone around here knows everyone.

MAI: No one sees a geeky Vietnamese girl and thinks, I wanna be her friend. I want to be part of her tribe.

DAVID: I wanna be part of your tribe.

MAI: You just want to have sex with me.

DAVID: True…

MAI: I can't wait till our A 'levels are over and we can get out of here.

They lie there in silence, smoking. DAVID puts his hand down her top. She lets him and enjoys it. They do this often.

DAVID: Do you think he killed anyone?

MAI: Who?

DAVID: Your dad.

MAI: Probably. Probably lots of people.

DAVID: What time do your parent's get home again?

They laugh.

DAVID: No serious, what time is it?

MAI: We have plenty of time.

They enjoy being with each other.

MAI: My dad likes the A team.

DAVID: Random.

MAI: The weird guy, what's his name?

DAVID: Murdoch?

MAI: Yeah, Murdoch.

He starts to hum the theme tune and MAI joins in.

MAI: It's fucking weird. You should go.

DAVID: What now?

MAI: Yeah, I want you to go.

DAVID: But we were just starting to/

MAI: To what?

DAVID: –

MAI: It's nearly eleven.

DAVID: Oh fuck, shit. You said there was plenty of time.

MAI: I know. I lied.

DAVID: What did you do that for?

MAI: I think I hear the door.

DAVID: What?

MAI: I'm only joking.

DAVID: Shit Mai, you gave me a heart attack.

MAI: I think you're more scared of my parents than I am.

DAVID: Do you really want me to go?

MAI: No…yes…no…no…you better go.

DAVID: Alright then.

MAI: –

DAVID: I'm going to go.

MAI: Yeah.

DAVID: I'll see you in class.

MAI: Hurry up and get out of here.

DAVID: Right yeah. Laters.

He quickly kisses her on the cheek. DAVID exits.

MAI immediately gets rid of remnants. Sprays air freshener, etc.

SCENE TWO

A Sunday. The family are eating dinner of braised pork belly and hot and sour soup. ANH reads a paper.

ANH: Listen to this:

'Every restaurant tells a story – but particularly compelling is the one about Summer Rolls. Anh Nguyen – helped out by mum –' they're talking about you, mum.

MOTHER: I know.

ANH: '– are introducing Pho to the frugal artistic East End community, and they can't get enough of it. Presenting recipes handed down from their grandmother…'

MOTHER: What did they say about your grandmother?

ANH: They say that grandmother taught you to cook.

MOTHER: Rubbish. Your grandmother didn't know how to cook. She had someone to do that for her. I made up all those recipes from up here.

MAI: Hurry up and get to the good bit will you.

MOTHER: Mai. Vietnamese.

MAI: –

MOTHER: What do they say about you, son?

ANH: 'Anh, who has a first class degree in mathematics, has turned a small derelict space, into a heart-warming place where you can sample the best of what Vietnamese food has to offer. And it has a lot to offer. I have a feeling that this is just the start.'

MOTHER: **The best.** You see. Everything I touch turns to gold. Only a few years of hard work and we've made it. Mr Dinh eat shit.

FATHER: Mai, get me some fish sauce.

MAI: Dạ ba.

(Yes father.)

MAI gets up and goes to fetch more fish sauce.

MOTHER: Fish sauce. The pork is already salty, why do you need fish sauce. If we left the restaurant to you, we'd be bankrupt by now.

ANH: We will have to hire more staff.

MOTHER: If you want to hire more staff, you should open on Sundays.

ANH: Open seven days?

MOTHER: What's wrong with that? We can rotate the staff so they each get a day off at the beginning of the week, when it's not too busy. Then we'll all be less tired at the weekends.

ANH: How about us?

MOTHER: You children. No head for business. Why would you want to make less profit when you don't have to.

ANH: But mother and father are already tired.

MOTHER: Son. We just have to suffer a little longer. Don't worry about me and your father. The important thing is to make money. Enough to buy you a place to live. Once you have that piece of land, no one can take it away from you. Mai can help out more if you need it.

MAI: A level của con sao?

(But how about daughter A-levels?)

MOTHER: One more evening won't kill you. Where do you think the money comes from to develop your pictures. When I was your age, I was selling broken rice on the street just so we wouldn't starve.

FATHER: Let the girl be.

MOTHER: Old man. Again with the defending.

ANH: If this girl doesn't want to help, don't force her.

MAI: I didn't say I didn't want to help.

There is a knock at the door.

MAI: Con mở cho.

(I'll get it.)

MAI leaves to get the door.

MOTHER: Probably Jahovas.

MR DINH: Hello Mai. Are your parents in?

MOTHER: Mr Dinh. What do you think he wants, old man?

FATHER: How would I know. I'm not a mind reader.

MOTHER: It's that review. I just know it.

Enter MR DINH. He is smaller than he was previously but still proud.

MOTHER: Mr Dinh. How's your health?

MR DINH: You're having dinner? I'll come back another time.

FATHER: Nonsense. Nonsense. Come in. Come in and join us.

MAI fetches him a bowl and chopsticks as he sits down

MR DINH: It looks delicious.

ANH: Hello Mr Dinh. How's your health?

MR DINH: I'm okay. I'm okay. Life is hard. You must know that. Being so busy and that.

MOTHER: You two, go check the stock ready to order.

ANH: Excuse me Uncle.

MR DINH: No Anh, you stay. I've come to see you too.

MOTHER: Mai. Upstairs.

MAI: Dạ me. Chào chú

(Yes mother. Bye uncle.)

She runs up to the loft room.

MR DINH: Each day she grows less and less like you old man.

FATHER: That's probably for the best.

MOTHER: Have you tried this pork? I'm thinking of putting it on the menu.

MR DINH: My son read the review to me. Sounds like you're doing very well.

MOTHER: God has blessed us. We have a lucky number.

FATHER: This old woman. Still so superstitious.

MR DINH: Nothing to do with experience. Just luck. Maybe that's where I'm going wrong. I should come round more often and hope your luck rubs off on me.

MOTHER: Some people are just born with it.

MR DINH: This pork is very good by the way. What do you put in it?

MOTHER: It's all about the tongue. You need to be able to taste the balance. There's an art to it.

MR DINH: Old man, I always knew you had a special woman.

MOTHER: I know this isn't a social visit. If you have something to say. Say it.

FATHER: Old woman. I'm sorry old man.

MR DINH: You have a face like leather you know that. If it wasn't out of respect for this old man I/

MOTHER: What? What would you do?

MR DINH: You stole my business from right under my nose. How can you sit here and act all innocent.

FATHER: What are you talking about?

MR DINH: You and your son act like you're angels but/

MOTHER: See the way he is, old man.

MR DINH: You are the devil.

FATHER: That's enough!

MOTHER: There. You see. I told you he was an evil communist. It's all coming out now.

MR DINH: If I had known I would never/

MOTHER: What? Let Anh do all the work while you put your feet up.

ANH: Mother don't/

MOTHER: I know how you bullied him. Made him do all the low work whilst you drank and / smoked.

ANH: That wasn't how /

MR DINH: You think too much of your son.

FATHER: Let's all calm down.

MOTHER: Do not tell me to calm down.

MR DINH: I should have known not to come here. I thought I could come and talk to you calmly.

MOTHER: Our son worked like a dog for him. Now we're doing a little better, he wants to come and ruin it for us.

ANH: Uncle. Say what you want to say and go.

MR DINH: The only reason you have anything is because of me.

MOTHER: You see, old man. See what I have to deal with?

MR DINH: You…you and your son. Stole my staff. Took my business. And now…now…

MOTHER: What? What are you trying to say?

MR DINH: Anh took care of the books and now the tax man is after me.

MOTHER: How dare you? How dare you come here and point the finger? Anh didn't do anything but help you.

ANH: Uncle, what's happened?

MR DINH: Old woman. How can you stand there and not feel guilt? You had a hand in this. I know you did.

MOTHER: You can think what you like. If it makes you feel better to blame someone else, then you do that. I have nothing to feel guilty about.

FATHER: Are you saying we had something to do with this?

MR DINH: Yes. Yes. That's exactly what I'm saying.

ANH and FATHER look at MOTHER.

MOTHER: Everyone knows. Everyone knows to hide a little cash here and there. If you're going to spend your cash on flashy cars, walk around like a big man, people are going to ask questions. This has nothing to do with me.

MR DINH: My wife told me not to come here. Said you were never going to let it rest. But I told her she was wrong. That you had suffered that's why you're so hard. That she shouldn't listen to gossip in the community. We're almost family. And family should stick together. Right old man?

FATHER: That's right.

MOTHER: Gossip? What gossip?

FATHER: Old woman.

MR DINH: I respect you, old woman. I respect your cunning and how you bring up your children so I don't care about the past. There is no gossip. Not unless you want there to be. It is time we came together now.

MOTHER: We will never be family.

ANH: Mother stop.

MR DINH: Be careful, old woman. I have been defending you in the community but I can go the opposite way.

MOTHER: You see, old man. Once a communist, always a communist.

MR DINH: Do you want Mai to know? It's about time she knew don't you think?

FATHER: What are you saying?

ANH: Keep your voices down. All of you. Uncle. I understand you're upset but there's no need for ugliness. What is it you want?

MR DINH: I didn't want it to come to this.

ANH: What do you need?

MR DINH: I could lose everything. Everything I've built.

ANH: Uncle, I will help you.

MR DINH: I still want Tuan and Mai to/

MOTHER: Never.

MR DINH: This is not easy for me.

ANH: Just say it.

MR DINH: The tax bill…I need money…

ANH: I'll take a look at the books and see what I can do.

MR DINH: Only until we're back on our feet.

FATHER: I think you should leave now.

MR DINH: Old man…this doesn't mean Tuan and Mai…

MOTHER: I would rather die than let my daughter marry your son.

FATHER: After all these years, I thought we could repair the cracks. I thought we could be Vietnamese together. But we are from different worlds.

MR DINH: Old man?

FATHER: On the outside our skin may be the same, but we have different blood running through our veins. Anh will help you, but I don't want to see your face here again.

MR DINH: –

MOTHER: You heard him.

ANH: I'll take you out uncle.

Exit MR DINH, led by ANH.

MOTHER: Old / man.

FATHER: Don't say anything.

MOTHER: We could not have married our daughter into that family.

Enter MAI.

MAI: Ai sắp cưới?

(Who's getting married?)

MOTHER: No one's getting married.

MAI: Ba mẹ la lối gì vạy?

(What were mother and father shouting about?)

MOTHER: Nothing.

FATHER: I'm going to bed.

Exit FATHER.

MOTHER: Did you check the stock?

MAI hands her MOTHER a shopping list.

Good. Tidy up here and turn the light off when you've finished.

MAI: Ba me có sao không?

(Father, mother, are you okay?)

MOTHER: Old woman Phan's daughter got straight A's at A level. Stop with that camera and study. We didn't bring you here for nothing.

Exit MOTHER. MAI tidies up in frustration.

SCENE THREE

Evening. Family home. There is giggling. Enter MAI and DAVID. They are drunk and merry.

MAI: That man was properly eyeing you up.

DAVID: Yeah man. He wanted a piece of this ass.

He shakes his ass, MAI laughs

MAI: I should have let you go in on your own, we might have got it for free.

She sits down, puts two envelopes on the table and starts rolling a spliff with ease.

DAVID: How do you get it so neat?

MAI: Lots and lots of practice. Summer rolls, summer rolls, summer rolls.

DAVID: You get the whiskey, I'll get the glasses.

MAI goes to fetch some glasses. He takes out the whiskey from a bag.

MAI: Ready?

They clink glasses and drink. She lights up and takes a drag. She passes it on.

What?

DAVID: Nothing.

MAI: You want me to go first?

DAVID: No. No. We'll open them together.

MAI: OK. Good idea. Mine.

She holds an envelope up and gives it to him

Yours.

She keeps one. Downs her drink.

DAVID: You've got no reason to be nervous.

MAI: Alright, after three.

DAVID: One, two, three!

MAI: One, two, three!

They open the envelopes together. Both take a moment to digest the information. They look at each other. DAVID reads her expression. He grabs it off her.

DAVID: Wicked! An A in music.

MAI: But…

DAVID: Who gives a shit about the other stuff.

MAI: I coached you in Maths.

DAVID: I'm sorry, is teacher disappointed in me?

MAI: How did I do?

He fakes a look. She grabs it off him.

You fucker!

DAVID: Told you, you didn't have anything to worry about. Professor Mai Nguyen. You pleased?

MAI: Mum will be.

DAVID: Maybe she'll be happy enough for you to tell her about me?

MAI: That's not going to happen.

DAVID: Why not?

MAI: Unless we're getting married, it's not worth the hassle.

DAVID: I'm not worth the hassle.

MAI: That's not what…

DAVID: Mai, you're going to Uni soon. You don't have to hide anymore?

MAI: You don't understand. They're not…I can't…

DAVID: What?

MAI: If you see them…and they don't accept you then/

DAVID: Mai, I can take that.

MAI: We'll be away from them soon. Can't you wait?

DAVID: I hate this hiding.

MAI pulls out her photos from under the sofa and shows them to DAVID.

What's this?

MAI: Photos.

DAVID: Of…

MAI: My parents.

DAVID: …your parents?

MAI: I don't have the words.

DAVID: They're…is this your mum?

MAI: I sometimes take them when he's sleepwalking. She comes and guides him back to bed.

DAVID: She looks…

MAI: Scary?

DAVID: No. I was going to say troubled. You look like her.

MAI: Is that supposed to be a compliment.

DAVID: They're beautiful.

MAI: I don't need you to approve them. I'm just showing you.

She takes them off him.

DAVID: Does it happen often?

MAI: No. I don't think so. They're not noisy. I just sense it. It's quiet. I can even hear my own heart beating when I'm taking them. I don't know. I seem to wake up when it's happening.

DAVID: They don't know you're watching them?

MAI: Nope.

DAVID: Mai, you really should talk to them.

MAI: It's a secret. Like everything in this house. When I bring it up with Anh, he says "You don't want to open up closed wounds".

DAVID: But have you even tried.

MAI: It's not that simple.

DAVID: How do you know until you start asking?

MAI: I don't know how…I have so much to say but I can't say it. When I speak Vietnamese it's like the sounds are choking me. I don't have the words. I feel closer to my parents looking at these photos than in real life.

DAVID: I'm sorry.

MAI: Everyone is always rushing around, busy making money, pretending it's all good. It stops when you put a camera on it.

He pulls her close.

DAVID: I didn't mean to pressure you.

MAI: It's not that I don't want to tell my parents about you. I would love to have them get to know you, but they don't even know me. Even if I wanted to, there isn't space for me to speak. As soon as I open my mouth my mum shuts me up. They want me to behave like this or like that, but it's like we're on different planets and I'm the alien. 'You're too young, You don't know how lucky you are' 'you owe it to your grandparents, people are suffering in Vietnam.' I know that. It's not my fault. Like their pain isn't my pain. Like I'm free from it. Instead they use it to control me.

DAVID: I don't think that's what they're doing.

MAI: How do you know. You don't know what it's like.

DAVID: You know, there are times when I want to ask my dad something and I can't. It always takes me a second or so to realise he's gone, and every time it feels like a hole has been blown through my stomach. I didn't really get a chance to know him. Properly you know. As a man, rather than just my dad. I was too scared to talk to him, a bit like you but not like you, if you know what I mean. He was always this far away figure that I couldn't touch, and then he died. I'm just saying.

MAI: This is different.

DAVID: They might surprise you.

MAI: How are you such an optimist? You know they won't react well to you.

DAVID: Not at first maybe.

MAI: You're really serious about this.

DAVID: Look, I've had to deal with racism all my life. But I know when things are worth fighting for.

Pause.

DAVID: Say something.

MAI: What?…No.

DAVID: Go on, please.

MAI: No. I don't want to.

DAVID: Please. It turns me on.

She smiles

MAI: Mắt Anh đẹp lăm.

(You have beautiful eyes.)

DAVID: Oh my god…poetry.

MAI: Chân Anh thúi vạy.

(Your feet smell.)

DAVID: What does it mean?

MAI: Ngày xửa ngay xưa có bà bán dừa.

(Once upon a time a woman sold coconuts.)

DAVID: You're so beautiful.

They kiss.

I should probably go…before…you know…

MAI: There's time.

She pulls him towards her.

Lights down.

SCENE FOUR

Same night. Midnight. MAI and DAVID are on the floor, passed out in an embrace. Half undressed. The aftermath of their party still around them. We hear the sound of a car pulling up.

DAVID: Mai, wake up. Wake up.

MAI: Mmmm.

DAVID: Wake up. Wake up. Your parents are home.

MAI: What?

DAVID: Your parents are home.

MAI: My parents are what?

DAVID: I think they're home.

MAI: What time is it?

DAVID: Midnight.

MAI: I thought you set the alarm clock.

DAVID: I thought you did!

MAI: Shit shit shit shit. What do we do. What do we do.

The door opens. They freeze. FATHER opens the door to the living room. Followed by MOTHER.

FATHER: What is this boy doing here?

MAI: Ba...

MOTHER: This girl! What have you been up to?

DAVID: Mrs/

MOTHER: Have you been doing dirty things in this house?

MAI: Không, không. không phải như vậy.

(No, no…it's not like that.)

MOTHER: My God, my god. You've been drinking?
And smoking?

DAVID: It's/

MOTHER: **Get out! You get out!**

DAVID: I/

MOTHER: Is this what you've been up to while we've been
working so hard. Whoring yourself out to dirty black
men?

DAVID: It/

MOTHER: Out!

DAVID: What?/

MOTHER: **What you do to my daughter?!**

DAVID: Wait. Hold on a minute.

She starts shoving him out of the door.

MAI: Mẹ, mẹ đừng làm vậy.

(Mum. Mum, don't do that.)

DAVID: Mrs Nguyen…

MOTHER: **Bastard, go! No, come back. You come back
I kill you!**

DAVID: I'm not…

MAI: Mẹ, đừng làm vạy

(Mum, don't do that!)

MAI grabs her MOTHER.

MOTHER: My God. Has it come to this?

MAI: Mẹ…

MOTHER: Everything we've done for you. Everything we've worked for. And you step over your mother for this black boy.

MAI: Không phải thằng đen. *(He's not black boy.)* His name is David.

MOTHER: What did you say?

MAI: Anh tên là David

(His name is David.)

MOTHER: It you! Out! Out! Get out, get out!

MAI: No David/ don't go.

DAVID: I should go.

MOTHER: Out! Out!

MOTHER grabs DAVID's arm whilst MAI grabs the other.

MAI: Leave him alone.

MOTHER: Get out!

MAI: Leave him alone.

FATHER: That's enough! How dare you talk to your mother like that?

MAI: Ba.

FATHER: Tell the boy to go home.

DAVID: I should really go.

MAI: No David please/

DAVID: This isn't…I'll call you tomorrow.

MAI: Don't go

FATHER: *(Calm.)* **David. Go home.**

DAVID: It's best I go. We'll talk soon.

He grabs his stuff.

Mr Nguyen. Mrs Nguyen…

He runs out.

MAI: Ba…

FATHER: Be quiet!

MAI: Ba…

FATHER: Your mother is right. You are a disobedient rotten child.

MAI: Mà co đâu có làm sai. Thật mà

(But I didn't do anything wrong. It's the truth.)

MOTHER: Now you've upset your father. Are you happy?

MAI: Ba…

FATHER: Get on your knees.

MAI: –

FATHER: On your knees. You have disgraced us. Disgraced me.

MAI: Nhưng mà…

(But…)

FATHER: Don't talk back to me. How dare you talk back to me!

MAI kneels. FATHER grabs a used feather duster leaning against the cupboard. He holds it at the top of the wooden handle like a cane to whip her with.

Put your arms out.

MAI: Ba…

FATHER: Put your arms out!

MAI does as she's told.

Don't you say a word. Don't talk. I loved you too much. Put too much trust in you. And this is how you repay us? I can't even look at you right now.

MAI: Ba…

FATHER starts to beat MAI with force. The beating coinciding with his words until he runs out of energy.

FATHER: You're rotten. I have to beat it out of you. Beat you till you bleed. You rotten rotten girl. You disgusting girl. No one's going to want you. No one's going to touch you. You're not my daughter. You're not my daughter. You belong in hell. I have to beat you…beat you…beat you…

MOTHER: Not so hard old man.

FATHER: You're not my daughter.

MOTHER: Not so hard.

FATHER: Woman, don't interfere. This is what you wanted isn't it. Isn't it?

MOTHER: Old man.

FATHER: Confess…

MAI: Ba…

FATHER: Confess…

MAI: Ba…

FATHER: You're not my daughter.

MOTHER: That's enough…

MAI: Ba…

FATHER: You did it…you confess…

MAI: …

MOTHER: Stop hitting her.

FATHER: Confess…confess…confess…

MOTHER: Old man… Stop hitting her. That's enough! That's enough!

ANH enters.

ANH: What is father doing?

He grabs the cane from his FATHER, who slumps exhausted.

Has father gone crazy?

FATHER: Tell her to go. Tell her she's no longer my daughter.

MOTHER: Old man.

FATHER: If we're not blood we're strangers.

MAI: Anh? Anh, what is he talking about?

ANH: Mai…

MAI: I want to know. Tell me. I want to know.

FATHER: You're a whore, just like your mother.

ANH: Don't say anymore. I won't let you say anymore.

MAI: Mẹ? Mẹ?

MOTHER can't reply. MAI understands. She gets up and runs out of the house.

MOTHER: Mai. Mai! Old man. Why do you have to destroy everything?

ANH: When son was small I watched you beat mother. I would hide in the corner of the house and cover my ears. I saw father hit mother again and again. Son couldn't stop you then but I won't let you beat Mai now.

MOTHER: This family is all I have. All I have in the world. You all want to hurt me that much. I've spent my whole life serving you. Serving your needs. Making sure you don't break and I'm tired old man. I'm so so tired.

She falls to the floor.

ANH: Stand up mother. Don't cry. Please don't cry.

MOTHER: I can't fix this.

ANH: Don't worry mother. I'll talk to her. She will be okay.

MOTHER: I can't fix this.

MOTHER picks up the A-level results from the floor.

MOTHER: Our daughter.

FATHER: Old woman.

MOTHER: Straight A's. What have you done?

He moves towards her.

ANH: Don't touch her.

FATHER leaves.

MOTHER: Anh. Go after her.

ANH reluctantly leaves.

INTERVAL

82

Act Three

SCENE ONE

1999. Family home. The TV has again got bigger. The family are having dinner. All are dressed smartly. No one is wearing an aó dài. It is MAI's graduation. They eat in silence until MAI finally speaks.

MAI: Ngon mẹ.

(Delicious, mother.)

ANH: Did you put shrimp paste in?

MOTHER: A tiny bit. I was scared this girl wouldn't cope with the smell.

MAI: Con can eat mắm tôm được mà.

(Daughter can eat shrimp paste sauce.)

MOTHER: You've never tasted real shrimp paste. The smell reaches the back of your throat. Anh knows, he remembers.

FATHER: Where's the rice?

MOTHER: If you want rice old man, cook it yourself.

FATHER: You need rice for a solid stomach.

MOTHER: If you want diabetes old man, then carry on. Mr Dinh nearly lost his foot because he couldn't stop eating.

MAI: How is Chú Đinh? *(To ANH.)*

ANH: Good.

MOTHER: Since you allow him to work for us, he's healthy.

Long pause.

MOTHER: Anh will help you move back home.

MAI: Con không về. Đừng bắt con.

(Daughter not coming home. Don't make daughter.)

MOTHER: It's up to your conscience.

FATHER: The girl is lost. Tuan is now married to a good Vietnamese girl. They're expecting a baby.

MAI: Ba…

(Father…)

FATHER: An unreligious daughter is a rotten daughter.

MAI: Con đâu làm gì sai.

(Daughter haven't done anything wrong.)

FATHER slams the table and his bowl drops on the floor. MAI goes to pick up the bowl.

FATHER: Leave it. I'm not hungry.

FATHER leaves. MOTHER gestures to for ANH to go after him.

MOTHER: Today was your graduation so I swallowed my words.

MAI: Con đâu muốn làm ba mẹ đau lòng.

(I don't want to hurt mother father feelings.)

MOTHER: If you don't want to hurt us, then come home.

MAI: Con không về.

(Daughter not coming home.)

MOTHER: When you were born, you tried to come out feet first. The midwife had to stick her hand in and turn you round. I screamed in agony. All I wanted was for you to live. I took care of every part of you daughter. I would stroke every strand of hair on your head, and soothe you with lullabies when you were hungry.

MAI: Mẹ.

MOTHER: When you had the pox, I stayed up every night to rub oil into your wounds. I prayed to God with every breath to save you, my daughter. My flesh and blood. Now you are a stranger.

Pause.

MAI: Mẹ muốn con làm sao?

(What do you want daughter to do?)

MOTHER: Get rid of him or you'll go to hell.

MAI: I can't.

MOTHER: **I can't.** What does that mean?

MAI: Con không biết nói.

(Daughter doesn't know how to say.)

MOTHER: You can't find the words because Vietnamese children don't talk back.

MAI: Con love David.

(Daughter love David.)

MOTHER: That doesn't last.

MAI: Con graduate, mẹ còn muốn gì nữa?

(Daughter graduated, what more does mother want?)

MOTHER: Your education is not for us. If you don't see that, then you're more stupid than I thought.

MAI: David là người tốt.

(David's a good person.)

MOTHER: Being a good person doesn't make him right for you.

MAI: All these years, ba mẹ vẫn gòn think like that.

(All these years, and mother father still think like that.)

MOTHER: Life is long and hard. Confess your sins and start again.

MAI: Không.

(No.)

MOTHER: Children go to university. Come back. Everything can be forgiven. People forget.

MAI: All you care about is what people think.

MOTHER: If you can't forget, you can't live.

MAI: Con không về not because I want to be with David. Con không về tại vì I can't breathe con không thở được in this house!

MOTHER: Do you know how much you have made your father suffer? Even after all the pain and embarrassment you've caused him, he still put on his suit for you to pick up a piece of paper. Your mother here is suffocating. I am suffocated by all of you.

MAI: Please mẹ.

MOTHER: I gave you freedom because I am forward thinking. I know the mind needs it. But you can't follow the English. You are Vietnamese. You have Vietnamese skin, Vietnamese nose, Vietnamese eyes, and the love of a Vietnamese family.

MAI: Con cannot pretend. I'm not responsible for the past.

MOTHER: My daughter is gone.

MAI: Mẹ.

Enter ANH. MOTHER sees him.

MOTHER: Just looking at this girl makes me want to cry.

MOTHER leaves. MAI starts to tidy up.

ANH: Leave that, I'll do it.

They tidy together.

MAI: That went well.

ANH: What did you expect.

MAI: How is dad?

ANH: The same.

MAI: I don't know how you live here?

ANH: We don't all have the luxury of leaving.

MAI: But you could if you wanted /

ANH: And go where?

MAI: Don't you want to meet someone?

ANH: When? Where?

MAI: Finding your own happiness is not selfish you know.

ANH: Making mum and dad unhappy isn't the way to find happiness.

MAI: You're twisting my words.

ANH: This whole family has worked hard in order for you to have the life that you have but you still can't see it.

You left for uni and turned yourself against the thing that makes you who you are.

MAI: You could have left too.

ANH: But I didn't.

MAI: David is the only true thing in my life.

ANH: Mum and dad are not cutting you off you know, you're doing it to yourself. If you want them to accept your life, maybe you should try understanding theirs.

MAI: Shouldn't it be both ways?

ANH: The other night, some drunk customers refused to leave. They started shouting "go home, you fucking foreigners" whilst they chucked money on the table and slurped our food. All mum kept saying was "thank you, thank you. Goodnight. Goodnight", all with a smile on her face.

MAI: What has this got to do with anything?

ANH: When dad got taken away to the camp, mum had to use all her resources to get by. She did everything she could so that I wouldn't starve. There are so many stories of people starving in Vietnam, but I don't remember ever being hungry.

MAI: Anh…

ANH: Family is everything. If I give in to my dreams, what would be left?

Pause.

MAI: Anh, I need to know who my real father is.

ANH: I don't know. I can't help you.

MAI: No one's saying anything.

ANH: Just let it go.

MAI: I can't.

ANH: You're not the only daughter who doesn't know who
    their father is. You think we're the only ones? Every
    refugee has a story. I had friends at the camp who never
    saw any of their family again. Some even committed
    suicide from loneliness. So please. Can you stop being so
    selfish.

MAI leaves. ANH finishes up tidying.

SCENE TWO

*Exhibition space. East London. There is a camera set up on a tripod.
A couple of fold-out chairs. MAI is there with DAVID checking her watch.*

MAI: I don't think he's going to come.

DAVID: You've always told me Vietnamese time was elastic.

They wait.

MAI: Do you believe in ghosts?

DAVID: What?

MAI: When I was younger I always felt someone was
    watching me.

DAVID: One spirit was always floating around my family.

MAI: I remember Mrs Le's daughter saying she felt her
    dead uncle stroke her face. They say that the beaches in
    Vietnam come alive at night with the spirits that have died
    at sea. The mist of unrestful souls.

DAVID: He'll be here.

MAI: I felt like an imposter going into those community
    centres. Seeing those older Vietnamese faces, it was like

having my whole history reflected at me. But when they spoke to me today, it was with such warmth.

DAVID: That's cause you're not their daughter.

MAI: I'm not sure I should be doing this.

DAVID: Mai, you need to do this.

MAI: Where do you think our child is going to see their histories reflected?

DAVID: Our child will have an abundance of cultures to choose and pick from.

MAI: It's not possible to know a culture unless you've lived it. I'm only beginning to discover where I'm from, and I can already feel it slipping away.

DAVID: Mai, you've not been able to speak to your parents for years. This is your way to heal, and maybe theirs too. Plus, we need to get to a point where you can tell your parents about the baby. This is a secret you can't keep.

Enter MR DINH. He looks like a fish out of water. MAI sees him. They reflexively jump away from each other.

MAI: Chào chú.

(Hello uncle.)

MR DINH: Mai.

MAI: Chú khỏe không?

(How's your health?)

MR DINH: I'm good. Good.

MAI: Chú, this David.

MR DINH: Ah David, **nice to meet you?**

DAVID: Nice to meet you too.

Pause.

I'll leave you to it.

DAVID leaves.

MR DINH: He seems nice.

MAI: Cám ơn chú for coming.

(Thank you, uncle, for coming.)

MR DINH: When I saw you at the community centre I was
surprised. Not many people of your age come. These
days, it's usually young children and old people.

MAI: Mời chú uống chà?

(Would uncle like tea?)

MR DINH: No. No tea. I'm fine.

She gets him some water. He takes it.

MR DINH: I'm sorry I'm late.

MAI: Không sao chú.

(No problem uncle.)

MR DINH: In truth, I wasn't sure if I should come.

MAI: Cháu very grateful chú đồng ý đến.

(Niece is very grateful uncle agreed to come.)

MR DINH: So…what do you want me to do? You know my
personality, I will try anything. Is this for TV?

MAI: No Chú.

MR DINH: Your parents told me you work in TV.

MAI: –

MR DINH: I'm teasing. I know what you do.

They smile.

MAI: Mời chú ngồi.

(Please, uncle, sit.)

MAI fetches him a chair and places him in front of the camera. He sits awkwardly.

MR DINH: I can see why your parents don't understand you. This is another world.

MAI: Chú có đồng ý cho cháu chụp hình chú không?

(Uncle, would you agree for niece to take pictures of you?)

He nods. She plays with the camera.

MR DINH: When I heard you were reaching out to the community I became curious.

MAI: Cháu just want người Việt an opportunity to tell their story. Xin lỗi chú, tiếng Việt cháu gần ngày gần tệ.

(I just want Vietnamese people an opportunity to tell their story. Sorry uncle. My Vietnamese is getting worse each day.)

MR DINH: Your Vietnamese is not bad. I can understand you. Lucky Tuan married a girl from Vietnam, otherwise he wouldn't be able to speak a single word. It's all worked out for the best. As sad as it made him, your heart was never going to be his…I'm saying, you're doing okay.

MAI: Chú có comfortable không?

(Are you comfortable uncle?)

He nods. Long silence.

MR DINH: I don't know what I should say.

MAI: Chú muốn nói bao nhiêu thì just say that.

(Uncle say as much as you want then just say that.)

MR DINH: It's not often you get to speak about the past. The words seem stuck.

MAI: Ba cháu khỏe không?

(How is my father's health?)

MR DINH: Your father misses you.

MAI: Ba cháu có nói gì về cháu không?

(Does father say anything about me?)

MR DINH: He doesn't say much. It's one of the reasons I'm here.

MAI: Tại sao ba cháu didn't come himself?

(Why didn't father come himself?)

MR DINH: If you have feet and can still use them, don't expect him to come to you.

MAI: Mà chú đến.

(But uncle came.)

MR DINH: I am not your father.

Pause.

MAI: Chú know ba mẹ cháu for as long as cháu can remember.

(Uncle has known mother father for as long as I can remember.)

MR DINH: A few decades now.

MAI: Chú có know ba mẹ ở Việtnam không?

(Uncle, did you know them in Vietnam?)

Pause.

MAI: I'm sorry chú. Cháu have to ask. Chú có biết gì về my real father không?

(I'm sorry, uncle. I have to ask. Uncle know anything about my real father?)

MR DINH: That is not my story to tell.

He gets up to leave.

MAI: Chú please.

(Uncle please.)

MR DINH: I want to help you.

MAI: Chàu always felt like I could talk to you.

MR DINH: But not this.

MAI: Không ai nói thật với cháu. Cháu lớn rồi. Please chú.

(No one will tell me the truth. I'm an adult. Please uncle.)

MR DINH: It was a long time ago.

MAI: Nếu chú remember anything, anything at all.

MR DINH: It's hard carrying the weight of the past, but you get used to it. Then you forget that you're heavier than you should be.

MAI: –

MR DINH: It was a long time ago.

MAI: Anything.

Pause. He sits.

MR DINH: When I was a young man, I was full of hope and
idealism. After the war ended, the faith in my country
was sucked out by the hole in my stomach. I watched my
mother starve to death. Still…I remember the day I heard
we stormed the presidential palace. The day we took our
country back was one of the happiest days of my life. I was
very young then. I had not been fighting for long but I felt
as if I was drunk on the best snake wine. Relief washed
over me. Around me, soldiers everywhere dropped their
weapons and rejoiced. Walking round the streets of Ho Chi
Minh…I don't know how long this drunken state lasted for.

MAI: Cháu didn't know you fought?

MR DINH: I didn't see the things your father saw.

MAI: Go on chú…

MR DINH: I needed to pee, so I found a small alley. As I
turned into it, a South Vietnamese soldier was stood there
pointing a gun at me. His hands were shaking. Eyes wide
and haunted. I said, "brother, the war is over. You can put
the gun down. Our country is united." Tears ran down his
cheeks like a waterfall. I will never forget his face. No one
moved for a long time. I knew he wasn't going to shoot
me but before I could do anything I heard the gunshot.
At first, I thought I'd been hit. Then I saw blood seeping
through his uniform. I caught him just before he hit the
ground. When I looked out of the alley, a fellow soldier
was standing there, his gun still up. I screamed for him to
help but he was afraid. There are no words to describe the
madness of it all. Blood was everywhere. Up close, it felt
like I was holding my brother dying in my arms. There
was nothing I could do. He pulled a crumpled photo from
his breast pocket and pressed it into my hand. 'Tell her I
love her,' he said. And then he went.

MAI: Chú…

MR DINH: I've never said that out loud.

MAI: −

MR DINH: There was a hand written name on the photo.
    I looked for her.

MAI: −

MR DINH: I asked around and found her in the city. She was
    carrying you. I never thought we would meet again.
    When your mother saw me in England, it was as if
    she's seen a ghost.

MAI: −

MR DINH: Your father doesn't know.

MAI: Mẹ cháu?

MR DINH: Your mother never forgave me.

MAI: Mẹ…

MR DINH: There was nothing I could have done.

MAI: −

MR DINH: I hope you can find peace Mai. I think it's time we
    all found peace.

The Exhibition – Part Two

MAI: …I…I hope this exhibition will in part help me, and other people of my generation to come together and mend these ruptures.

During this journey, I have come to a deeper understanding of myself through the memories of others. I would like you to take yourselves on your own journey through these pieces.

What is art for, if not to remember. These people are not heroes, or anti- heroes. They are just ordinary people, to whom extraordinary things have happened.

Thank you for listening.

FATHER steps forward

MAI: Ba.

(Father.)

FATHER: You've got fat.

MAI: –

FATHER: I hope you're lighter on your feet these days.

MAI: –

FATHER: You're heavy-footed. The baby can hear everything. You need to walk softer.

MAI: Ba đứng đó bao lâu vậy?

(How long have you been standing there?)

FATHER: Long enough to hear your speech.

MAI: Ba làm sao tìm thấy con?

   (How did father find daughter?)

FATHER: Internet.

MAI: Ba dùng internet?

FATHER: Old man Dinh.

MAI: –

FATHER: He told me he came to see you.

   Pause.

FATHER: So this is what you do?

MAI: Ba nghĩ sao?

   (What does father think?)

FATHER: They're pretty pictures.

MAI: It's more than that.

FATHER: **Speak English. It better for you.** I can understand.

MAI: Con đang cố gắng nói tiếng Việt.

   (I'm trying hard to speak Vietmamese.)

FATHER: This one is good. No veil over the eyes. Most of them are still protecting themselves, can you see?

MAI: People see what they want to see.

FATHER: People pay to see these?

MAI: Nó giúp người ta remember

   (It helps people to remember.)

FATHER: These people, they drink with their eyes and then piss it out.

MAI: Sao ba tới vậy?

(Why did father come here?)

FATHER: When were you going to tell us about the baby?

MAI: Con wanted to tell you. Con just/

FATHER: You were scared.

MAI: No. Ashamed.

FATHER: It is not the way we would have wanted, but a new life is something to celebrate.

MAI: The longer con left it, the harder it got.

FATHER: We have not made it easy for you. I accept that.

Pause.

MAI: I know I've been a bad daughter.

FATHER: Why didn't you come home?

MAI: Con didn't know what to say.

FATHER: You know, when I first saw you, you were already walking. This little tiny thing. You came up to me and grabbed my finger. Pulled me towards the mango tree in the garden and pointed.

He laughs.

From that moment, I knew. You would know what you wanted from life.

MAI: Ba…

FATHER: I haven't always been a good man. Your mother has tried her best. We all make mistakes.

MAI: Ba don't have to explain.

FATHER: Those lines get blurred very easily when you've been through a war. This is good a good way. *(Pointing at the pictures.)*

Pause.

These people. You talk to them?

MAI: Dạ.

FATHER: That's good. Your mother needs you. She's sick. She needs a woman. To do woman things. Things I can't do.

MAI: Why didn't anyone tell me sooner?

FATHER: You know your mother. Usually she's a loud mouth, but this time she kept it quiet. You're going to be a mother soon. You'll understand. We're all just flesh and bones underneath it all.

MAI looks at DAVID, who has been in the background waiting to step in.

Bring David too.

MAI: I missed you, ba.

Pause.

FATHER: There's a picture missing from this exhibition. Come home and you can put a story to it.

SCENE THREE

Family home. The living room has been turned into a bedroom. MOTHER has deteriorated substantially. She is lying in a hospital bed slightly upright. FATHER is tenderly feeding her soup. Even in ill health, she gives the impression of strength.

MOTHER: Old man, just me and you. Look at you feeding me soup.

FATHER: Shhh, eat don't talk. Eat.

MOTHER: When I'm not here, who's going to take care of you? And the children? They still need so much help.

FATHER: We can take care of ourselves.

MOTHER: What about Anh? What about the restaurant?

FATHER: He'll be fine.

MOTHER: He's so angry these days.

FATHER: You shouldn't worry about him. He's a grown man.

MOTHER: He needs a wife.

FATHER: He'll find one in his own time.

MOTHER: You two need to look after each other when I'm gone. No arguing.

FATHER: Enough woman.

MOTHER: And Mai? What about Mai? She's just like you. Stubborn.

FATHER: Old woman, stop talking so much. You're on your deathbed and you still won't shut up.

MOTHER: When you're young you think you don't need anybody. Then when you're old, there's nobody there.

She shuffles.

FATHER: What's wrong?

MOTHER: I need to pee.

FATHER: Right now.

MOTHER: –

FATHER: Okay. Hold on.

> *He puts the soup down and gets a metal pan. She holds onto him as he lifts her up. She shuffles her knickers off under the covers and he puts the pan under her. She relieves herself. He takes it away.*

Would you like any more soup?

MOTHER: No. no.

He tidies up.

MOTHER: Old man?

FATHER: Yes.

MOTHER: Do you think God will take care of me?

FATHER: When you feel bleak, or alone, pray and he will comfort you.

MOTHER: Old man…I'm frightened.

FATHER: There's no need.

MOTHER: I'm really frightened.

FATHER: Shhhhhh I'm here with you. I'm here.

Doorbell rings.

FATHER: Wait here.

MOTHER: I'm not going anywhere.

He re-enters with MAI.

MAI: Mẹ

MOTHER: Mai?

MAI: Mẹ

MOTHER: You're here. Come here. Come here daughter.

MAI: Mẹ, con xin lỗi, con xin lỗi mẹ.

(Mother, I'm sorry, I'm sorry.)

MOTHER: Eh, what is there to be sorry for? You've come
to visit.

MAI: Mẹ.

MOTHER: What is wrong with you? You're acting like I've
already gone.

MAI: Tại sao mẹ không nói cho con biết. Nếu con biết…

)Why did mother not let me know. If daughter knew…)

MOTHER: I didn't want you to worry. You have your life…

MAI: Con không biết tại sao why con scared to come …

(Daughter doesn't know why I was so scared to come…)

MOTHER: This girl. A mother's love is endless like a
mountain river. You know that. I told you enough times.
Look at your mother. So messy.

MAI: Mẹ đừng lo, you look beautiful.

(Mother don't worry, you look beautiful.)

MOTHER: This girl, something wrong with your eyes? Stand
up. Let me look at you.

MAI: –

MOTHER: What is this? Is this right?

MAI: Dạ mẹ.

MOTHER: A grandchild?

MAI: Dạ.

MOTHER: You were pregnant and you didn't tell me?

MAI: Con không biết how.

(Daughter didn't know how.)

Pause.

MOTHER: Old man. Have you seen?

FATHER: You can see it from space.

MOTHER: We're going to be grandparents.

She laughs.

MAI: Mẹ không angry ha?

(Mother's not angry?)

MOTHER: You knew and you didn't tell me.

FATHER: I didn't know how.

MOTHER: What do you mean you didn't know how. You open your mouth and say it.

MAI: Con nói ba đừng nói.

(Daughter told father not to say.)

MOTHER: Where is he then? Where is that black boy?

MAI: Mẹ, he has a name.

MOTHER: Okay okay, where is David?

MAI: Anh ở ngoài mẹ.

(He's outside, mother.)

MOTHER: Well tell him to come inside. He took my daughter away, the least he could do is look me in the eye. Old man, you go.

FATHER leaves to get DAVID.

Is he looking after you? You know you have your child to care for now. Men can come and go, but you are always a mother.

MAI: You don't need to worry about him. Concentrate on getting better.

MOTHER: Are you married?

MAI: Mẹ này.

MOTHER: Okay. Okay. I'm only asking.

MAI: Tụi con okay

(We are okay.)

MOTHER: You young are always fine. You have to plan for the future. Like me. I'm always ready, no matter what happens.

FATHER re-enters with DAVID.

DAVID: Chào bác

(Hello auntie.)

MOTHER: You taught him Vietnamese?

MAI: Không mẹ. He taught himself.

MOTHER: **You, look at me. If you no look after her, I come back from the dead, and kill you.**

MAI: Mẹ!

MOTHER: It's okay. It's okay. I'm only joking.

MOTHER laughs and starts to cough.

FATHER: You're getting yourself all excited again woman.

MOTHER: How can I not be excited.

MAI: Mẹ, try not to talk too much.

MOTHER: If I don't talk, what am I going to do. Die?

MAI: Mẹ.

MOTHER: This girl. I'm joking. When did you get so serious. Or have you always been like this…Your baby is going to be so beautiful. Anything mixed with the Vietnamese gene is beautiful. Does David know how lucky he is.

MAI: He knows mum.

She takes out a rosary from under her pillow.

I want you to have it.

MAI: Mẹ?

MOTHER: For you to pray. With your father. When I'm gone.

Pause.

Now you're here. Fetch that brush? Your father's useless. I've missed having another woman in the house.

MAI picks up the brush from the side table and starts brushing MOTHER's hair. MOTHER closes her eyes and enjoys the sensation. FATHER gestures to DAVID for them to leave.

MOTHER: You know daughter, each person suffers in their own way.

MAI: Con biết.

(Daughter knows.)

MOTHER: I'm sorry that I pushed mine onto you.

MAI: Mẹ đừng nói…

(Mother don't speak…)

MOTHER: Let me speak. You and your father want to use my illness to stop shut me up.

MAI: –

MOTHER: When you have time, you must spend time with your brother.

MAI: Dạ mẹ

MOTHER: Your brother as done so much. He needs looking after.

MAI: I know mum.

MOTHER: And your father.

MAI: Dạ mẹ.

MOTHER: You're the woman of this house now. A strong woman. Like me.

MAI: I'm will never be as strong as you mum.

MOTHER: Stronger. I should have told you about your father.

MAI: Shhhhh you don't have to.

MOTHER: I should have told you.

MAI: Con know mum. Chú Đinh nói con.

(Daughter know mum. Uncle Dinh told daughter.)

MOTHER: He/...

MAI: Chú told me everything.

(Uncle told me everything.)

MOTHER: I didn't mean for it to happen. I was on my own.
He was so kind to me. And handsome.

MAI: Mẹ?

MOTHER: The women in this house are the same. When we
love, we love with all of ourselves. Mr Dinh was there. He
was there when he died.

MAI: Con biết.

(I know.)

MOTHER: I never forgave him. I've been brittle.

MAI: Thôi mẹ ngủ đi.

(Mother go to sleep.)

MOTHER: How could I have been so brittle. He's a
good man.

MAI: Con biết.

(Daughter knows.)

MOTHER: Your father doesn't know.

MAI: Con không nói. Don't worry mẹ.

(Daughter won't say. Don't worry mother.)

MOTHER starts to fall asleep.

MOTHER: It'll be our secret.

MAI: Shhhhh.

MOTHER: Remember…

MAI: Con remember.

MOTHER: Your father told me about your exhibition.

She sleeps. We hear 'Long Me' on the flute.

SCENE FOUR

FATHER, MR DINH and DAVID are playing cards.

BBC NEWS BROADCAST: 'Massive ground assault is underway. The Americans warn it is just a taste of things to come. Dozens of cruise missiles fired at targets including the home of Saddam Hussein. More on the way. Here in Britain, America's B52 prime for action. And the prime minister, now confirms Britain's involvement.'

FATHER: Bloody Americans.

MR DINH: Now it's bloody Americans.

FATHER: Their war ends, but the country they ravage have to live in the aftermath. If it's not Vietnam it's some other poor country.

MR DINH: I thought you didn't do politics.

FATHER: I don't. A person just can't escape it.

MR DINH: You speak the truth my friend. You speak the truth.

FATHER: I win again.

MR DINH: Fuck your mother, I'm sure you're cheating.

DAVID: Wait is it finished?

MR DINH: **David, this man is a cheat.**

DAVID: I'm sorry uncle, I can't say anything against my kids grandfather

FATHER: I have him well trained.

DAVID starts dealing cards.

MR DINH: I never thought I'd see the day you would be living in the same house as the black boy.

FATHER: The feel is different, but I'm getting used to it.

DAVID: Are you talking about me again?

MR DINH: **No, we're just talking.**

DAVID: I can understand more than I can say you know.

FATHER: **I would never say anything against my daughters husband.**

DAVID: We're not married yet Mr Nguyen.

FATHER: **You will be.**

MR DINH: I don't understand why this generation is so scared of marriage.

FATHER: I will never understand anything they do.

MR DINH: How are you coping old man?

FATHER: The baby is keeping us all busy. There's no time to think.

MR DINH: I'm sure the old woman is smiling down on you.

FATHER: Just because she's dead, doesn't mean she will change.

MR DINH: Ha! Yes.

They laugh.

DAVID: What's the joke?

FATHER: **You wouldn't get it.**

They laugh some more. Enter MAI.

MAI: David, can you help Anh load the rest of his stuff?

DAVID: My pleasure.

FATHER: **We no talk about you. I promise.**

DAVID: It's okay uncle. No offence taken.

He mimes to MAI that he is wounded and leaves. Enter ANH.

MR DINH: I better get out of here too. The restaurant can't look after itself.

ANH: If uncle need anything, uncle can call me.

MR DINH: What are you going to do from the other side of the world.

ANH: Thank you uncle. For everything.

MR DINH: No need to thank me. Just make sure you bring back a wife.

ANH: That's not the reason I'm going.

MR DINH: People never go for that reason, but they always seem to come back with one. Isn't that right old man.

FATHER: That's right.

MR DINH: Maybe we could go back to Vietnam together one day.

FATHER: Maybe one day. With my granddaughter.

We hear a baby cry.

FATHER: There! She's got the old woman's super hearing. Take care Mr Dinh.

MR DINH: Take care old man. Mai. Have a good journey.

The two men exit, leaving MAI and ANH on their own.

MAI: I can't believe you won't be living here anymore.

ANH: You can re-decorate. Make it look all fancy.

MAI: Quite hard to make this place look fancy.

ANH: I'm sure you can do it. This area is changing.

MAI: Do you remember what a shithole it was when we first arrived.

ANH: The carpet was a horrible brown, but it meant that we could spill stuff and mum wouldn't notice.

MAI: Mum noticed everything.

ANH: I've often wondered what our lives might have been like if we'd stayed in Vietnam? The place has become a backpackers paradise now. We could be hoteliers if we'd stayed.

MAI: Bet mum would have loved that.

ANH: She could probably own half of Saigon. Here she could only do so much.

MAI: Well, you'll see for yourself now.

ANH: –

MAI: I got you something.

ANH: Oh no Mai, what?

MAI: It's nothing big.

She takes out a framed photo of MOTHER caught unawares.

I thought you might want it.

ANH: When she was alive, I thought she needed me to protect her. I think that's why I never left. But it was the other way round. I was terrified of losing her. Now she's gone…I guess I'm free.

DAVID: The car's all packed. We better go if were want to beat the traffic.

ANH: Thank you little sis.

They hug.

MAI: Aren't you going to say goodbye to dad?

He shakes his head.

ANH: He knows.

They exit, leaving MAI by herself.

All is quiet for a moment, then the sound of a baby crying.

She runs upstairs.

The sound continues into the epilogue.

Epilogue

Vietnam 1980. Sparse living space. A baby is crying in the background.

WOMAN: Husband.

MAN: Every day I would pray for the time when I could see you and Anh again. Each time they promised they'd release me, they didn't. Days turned to months, months into years. I lost time.

WOMAN: You left me.

MAN: We were at war.

WOMAN: I didn't think you were coming back.

MAN: You mean you wished I was dead.

WOMAN: I prayed for you every day. I had our son to look after.

MAN: And the girl?

WOMAN: Her father was a good man.

MAN: You expect me just to accept?

WOMAN pulls out a letter and starts to cry.

WOMAN: Anh made it husband. He made it.

MAN: What are you talking about woman?

WOMAN: I thought the sea had taken him. But I prayed. I prayed for a a thousand years and my prayers were answered. Anh made it to England.

MAN: England?

WOMAN: This is his letter. We can leave this place.

MAN: What would I do in England?

WOMAN: Build a new life.

MAN: I don't know how to.

WOMAN: You have a daughter.

MAN: I am not her father.

WOMAN: We can start again. In a land where we are free to live without fear.

MAN: I do not know if I have the strength.

WOMAN: I have enough for all of us.

MAN: What does freedom look like?

WOMAN: Choice.

MAN: And?

WOMAN: Peace.

MAN: We will be free.

WOMAN: We will be free.

THE END

www.ingramcontent.com/pod-product-compliance
Ingram Content Group UK Ltd.
Pitfield, Milton Keynes, MK11 3LW, UK
UKHW020714280225
455688UK00012B/355

9 781786 828040